Speaking of
HORROR

INTERVIEWS WITH WRITERS OF THE SUPERNATURAL

by Darrell Schweitzer

CONTENTS

DEDICATION

*For STEVE BEHRENDS,
perceptive delver into
the eldritch and infinite*

INTRODUCTION

The writers interviewed in this volume are all leading practitioners of modern horror fiction. By "modern" I mean post-Lovecraftian, for all that the late Manly Wade Wellman published from the 1920s to his death in 1986 (and beyond with posthumous material) and Robert Bloch was a disciple of Lovecraft. Horror fiction as it is practiced today has turned away from the direction in which Lovecraft was pointing, away from the abstract and cosmic, toward the personal and psychological. At the same time, the prose has gotten more straightforward.

This is not to deny the influence of Lovecraft. Indeed, most of these interviews deal in part with the writers' reactions to Lovecraft, even if this has been to remove themselves as far from the Lovecraftian tradition as possible. In the process a new, distinctly different tradition has emerged, which can reach and speak to (and scare into delicious hysteria) a lot of people. It's an infrequent week in which there isn't at least one horror novel in the contemporary tradition on the bestseller lists.

Here are conversations with some of the people who have made the field of horror what it is today.

—Darrell Schweitzer
Strafford, Pennsylvania
28 August 1993

ILLUSTRATIONS

The author would like to thank the following people who generously provided the photos used in this book:

SPEAKING OF HORROR

Interviews with Writers of the Supernatural

I.

ROBERT BLOCH

A ROBERT BLOCH CHRONOLOGY

1917 Robert Albert Bloch born April 5 at Chicago, Illinois.

1932 Begins correspondence with H. P. Lovecraft.

1934 "Lilies" published in *Marvel Tales* (semiprozine), Winter.

1935 "The Feast in the Abbey" published in *Weird Tales*, January (first professional publication); "The Secret in the Tomb" (first professional sale, accepted earlier) appears in *Weird Tales*, May; "The Shambler from the Stars" (in which Bloch kills off a thinly-disguised H. P. Lovecraft) in *Weird Tales*, September; "Black Lotus" published in *Unusual Stories* (semiprozine), Winter.

1936 "The Grinning Ghoul" published in *Weird Tales*, June; "The Opener of the Way" appears in *Weird Tales*, October; "Mother of Serpents" published in *Weird Tales*, December; Lovecraft retaliates for "The Shambler from the Stars" by killing off young author ROBERT BLAKE in "The Haunter of the Dark," in *Weird Tales*, December.

1937 H. P. Lovecraft, Bloch's friend and mentor, dies, March 15; "The Mannikin" published in *Weird Tales*, April.

1938 "The Secret of the Observatory" (first science fiction story) published in *Amazing Stories*, August; "Return to the Sabbath" appears in *Weird Tales*, July.

1939 "The Strange Flight of Richard Clayton" published in *Amazing Stories*, March; "The Cloak" published in *Unknown*, March.

1940 Marries Marion Holcombe.

1941 "A Good Knight's Work" published in *Unknown Worlds*, October.

1942 Advertising Copywriter, Gustav Marx Advertising Agency (until 1953); LEFTY FEEP series begins with "Time Wounds All Heels," *Fantastic Adventures*, April.

1943 "Yours Truly, Jack the Ripper" published in *Weird Tales*, July.

1945   Adapts thirty-nine of his stories for radio program *Stay Tuned For Terror*; "The Skull of the Marquis de Sade" published in *Weird Tales*, September; *The Opener of the Way* (first collection) published by Arkham House.

1946   "Enoch" published in *Weird Tales*, September; "Lizzie Borden Took an Axe" published in *Weird Tales*, November.

1947   First novel, *The Scarf*, published by Dial.

1948   Guest of Honor, Torcon I, World Science Fiction Convention, Toronto, Canada.

1950   Last LEFTY FEEP story, "End of Your Rope," published in *Fantastic Adventures*, July.

1952   "Lucy Comes to Stay" published in *Weird Tales*, January.

1954   *The Kidnapper* published by Lion; *Spiderweb* and *The Will to Kill* published by Ace.

1958   *Shooting Star* and *Terror in the Night and Other Stories* published by Ace.

1959   *Psycho* published by Simon & Schuster; wins Hugo Award for "That Hellbound Train"; "Imagination and Modern Social Criticism," lecture delivered at the University of Chicago, reprinted in *The Science Fiction Novel* (Advent); "The Hungry Eye" published in *Fantastic*, May.

1960   *The Dead Beat* published by Simon & Schuster; first television script sales to *Alfred Hitchcock Presents*, *Thriller*, *Lock-Up*, etc., often adapting Bloch's stories; *Psycho* made into film by Alfred Hitchcock (Bloch not involved); *Pleasant Dreams—Nightmares* published by Arkham House.

1961   *Firebug* published by Regency; wins special Mystery Writers of America Scroll for *Psycho*; *Blood Runs Cold* published by Simon & Schuster.

1962   *The Couch* published by Fawcett; film of *The Couch* with screenplay by Bloch, Owen Crump, and Blake Edwards released; *Atoms and Evil* published by Gold Medal; *Terror*, *More Nightmares*, and *Yours Truly, Jack the Ripper* (collection) published by Belmont; screenplay of *The Cabinet of Dr. Caligari*; *The Eighth Stage of Fandom: Selections from 25 Years of Fan Writing* (collection of Bloch's fanzine material) edited by Earl Kemp, published by Advent.

1963   Divorces Marion; *Bogey Men* published by Pyramid; *Horror-7* published by Belmont.

1964   Marries Eleanor Alexander; writes screenplays *The Night Walker* and *Strait-Jacket*.

1965   *The Skull of the Marquis de Sade* (collection) and *Tales in a Jugular Vein* published by Pyramid.

1966 Wins Ann Radcliffe Award for Television; *Chamber of Horrors* published by Award; screenplay, *The Psychopath*, and three *Star Trek* teleplays produced (1966-67).

1967 *The Living Demons* published by Belmont; writes screenplays *The Deadly Bees* (with Anthony Marriott), *Torture Garden*; "A Toy for Juliette" published in *Dangerous Visions*, edited by Harlan Ellison, Doubleday.

1968 *This Crowded Earth and Ladies' Day* published by Belmont; *The Star Stalker* published by Pyramid; *Dragons and Nightmares* published by Mirage Press.

1969 Wins Ann Radcliffe Award for Literature; *Bloch and Bradbury* published by Tower; *The Todd Dossier* (as COLLIER YOUNG) published by Delacorte.

1970 Screenplay, *The House That Dripped Blood*.

1971 Serves as president of Mystery Writers of America; *Sneak Preview* published by Paperback Library; *Fear Today, Gone Tomorrow* published by Award; *It's All In Your Mind* published by Curtis.

1972 *Night-World* published by Simon & Schuster; writes screenplay, *Asylum*.

1973 Guest of Honor, Torcon II, World Science Fiction Convention, Toronto, Canada; writes teleplay for *The Cat Creature* (ABC Movie of the Week).

1974 *American Gothic* published by Simon & Schuster.

1975 Wins World Fantasy Award for Life Achievement.

1976 Two records of Bloch readings, *Gravely Robert Bloch* and *Blood!* (with Harlan Ellison) released by Alternate World Recordings; *House of the Hatchet* (British reprint of *The Opener of the Way*) published by Panther.

1977 *The Best of Robert Bloch* edited by Lester del Rey, published by Del Rey Books; *Cold Chills* appears from Doubleday; *The King of Terrors* released by Mysterious Press.

1978 *Strange Eons* published by Whispers Press.

1979 *There Is a Serpent in Eden* published by Zebra; *Out of the Mouths of Graves* published by Mysterious Press; *Such Stuff as Screams Are Made of* published by Del Rey.

1980 *The First World Fantasy Convention* (with T. E. D. Klein & Fritz Leiber) published by Necronomicon Press.

1981 *Mysteries of the Worm* published by Zebra.

1982 *Psycho II* (no relation to film of same title) published by Warner and Whispers Press.

1983 *The Twilight Zone: The Movie* (novelization of screenplay) published by Warner.

1984 *The Night of the Ripper* published by Doubleday.

1986 *Unholy Trinity* published by Scream Press (collects *The Scarf*, *The Dead Beat*, and *The Couch*); *Out of My Head* published by NESFA Press.

1987 Celebrates 70th birthday. *The Selected Stories of Robert Bloch* (3 vols.: *Final Reckonings*, *Bitter Ends*, *Last Rites*) published by Underwood-Miller; *Midnight Pleasures* published by Doubleday; *Lost in Time and Space with Lefty Feep* published by Creatures At Large (first of three projected volumes; the other two have not appeared).

1988 *The Kidnapper* published by Tor.

1989 *Fear and Trembling* and *Lori*, published by Tor; *The Robert Bloch Companion* (with Randall D. Larson) published by Starmont House; *Screams* published by Underwood-Miller (collects *The Will to Kill*, *Firebug*, and *The Star Stalker*).

1990 *The Jekyll Legacy* (with Andre Norton) and *Psycho House* (the third Norman Bates novel) published by Tor.

1991 Special Robert Bloch issue of *Weird Tales*, Spring; *Yours Truly, Jack the Ripper* published by Pulphouse; *Psycho-Paths* (edited with Martin H. Greenberg) published by Tor.

1992 Celebrates 75th birthday with a bash at a Los Angeles mystery/horror bookstore with many notables from the fields of horror & SF attending.

1993 Publication of "unauthorized autobiography," *Once Around the Bloch* (Tor).

1994 *The Early Fears*, collection of 39 stories, published by Fedogan & Bremer.

A ROBERT BLOCH INTERVIEW

SCHWEITZER: You're the only one of the *Weird Tales* group to have any experience in Hollywood. How did that come about?

BLOCH: It came about because of a man I knew who was already in television (who has always strongly objected to my using his name, because when I did that once he was inundated with requests from people to do the same). At any rate, in 1959 he called me up and asked me if I could do a segment of a television show to which he had sold many segments—a syndicated show. It was a detective show without any particular violence in it, and he said I might have a chance to do pretty much what I wanted, because I had resisted doing westerns and that sort of thing which were then in vogue. He said, "Come out to the house and stay with me for two or three weeks or however long it takes to do the script. I made an arrangement with the producer so that you will get the Guild's minimum fee for writing the script, and if they don't like your work, I will back it up and replace it with a script of my own and I get the highest fee, and they'll still get it for the lowest price." He said the best that could happen was that I would find out I could write for television, and the worst that could happen would be that I'd have three weeks of vacation. It was a wonderful offer.

I went out there and got the assignment and came up with the story. I felt that there was no point at all in my asking him for advice or criticism or help because this wouldn't teach me anything. I would have to see if I could do it on my own. I wrote a script and turned it in. They immediately asked for a second one. I did the second one, and by this time I had acquired an agent, moved into a little apartment of my own, and decided to send for my family. However, no sooner had I made this decision than the Writers Guild had a strike, during which time you are not allowed to write. I had multiple assignments from various television companies, but I was not allowed to write for television for five months. So I sat and wrote more fiction. Then the strike was over and I finished the scripts, went back to the Midwest, collected my family, came out, and from then on I was writing for television.

Almost immediately I was approached and asked if I could do a film. Meanwhile, Alfred Hitchcock had filmed something called *Psycho*, but this had no part whatsoever in my coming to Hollywood. By the time it was released, I already had my first film offer, so it had nothing to do with that. In fact, prior to its release everybody thought it was going to be a tremendous bomb, and Hitchcock had great trouble in getting it produced. He had the right to choose his own story material, but Paramount didn't care for the subject matter, so they cut his budget. He'd been using big stars like Cary Grant and Jimmy Stewart and Grace Kelly in his films, and Kim Novak who was very popular at that time, and doing them all in technicolor. But this time he was only able to afford black and white with lesser players and the services of the cameraman, John Russell, who did his television series shooting. And they wanted him to change the title, and Paramount wasn't able to find room for him on Paramount's lot—he had to shoot the film at Universal, and it was quite a mess. Then it came out and everybody started to take bows, and from that time on everybody assumed that I went out to Hollywood because of *Psycho*. That was not the case.

SCHWEITZER: When did you get into doing horror films, supernatural films?

BLOCH: Well, immediately...or almost immediately. I had been approached by the Hitchcock television show to do some episodes, and a year later, a show called *Thriller* came on the air. Boris Karloff was the host and I did quite a few of those. So I had perhaps a dozen *Hitchcocks* and a dozen *Thrillers* to my credit. Meanwhile the films started to come in the genre.

SCHWEITZER: Did you have any problems with artistic freedom, things like people chopping up your scripts until you didn't recognize them?

BLOCH: Oh, yes! Most of the time. In the film area, this is par for the course. This is one of the hazards, one of the things you have to accept. This is why so many writers become writer-directors or writer-producers, so they can have some autonomy, or shoot abroad, where they're not being supervised by studio production people who watch the dailies and make changes as they go along.

Television, initially *Hitchcock* and *Thriller*, gave me the greatest freedom. They made some changes, but the changes were the result of constructive criticism on the part of producers of the shows, who knew the fields in which they

13

worked, and who could give a "yes" or "no" answer. But along about the mid-1960s, the networks took over. Now the producers, by and large—with one or two exceptions in the comedy field, people who have runaway hits like Norman Lear—and the story editors have no real control at all. They can tell you they like something, then sit down, phone New York, and get approval of it, and the changes come from New York. What the writer hears when he goes in is "They don't like this. They want this done," or "They would like to have you rewrite." You never meet "They" because They are somewhere back East at the other end of the telephone line, so you're being tried and condemned by an invisible judge and jury.

SCHWEITZER: When you did that *Star Trek* script, the Halloween one, how much of the final product resembled what you had written?

BLOCH: I would say perhaps sixty percent, which is a pretty good percentage by the standards of that day and today.

SCHWEITZER: Do you find enough artistic satisfaction in Hollywood to stick it out?

BLOCH: Well, I'll tell you, I'm not so much interested in artistic satisfaction as I am in some other aspects. Number one: a writer likes to have an audience and to communicate. Certainly this is the biggest audience. This is the biggest ball game in the whole business. There is a certain satisfaction in reaching more people, even though you may not be able to reach them in exactly the fashion you want to. Secondly, I've always been a motion picture fan. That goes back to the 1920s, when I was like millions and millions of other kids in that era, a movie-goer two and three times a week. I'm still a fan, and I got such a thrill out of coming out to Hollywood and meeting some people that I'd seen on the screen as a child, and because I'd seen them so many times I felt I knew them better than some of my own relatives. I never thought I would meet or have any friendship with people like Buster Keaton and Joan Crawford and Barbara Stanwyck and Robert Taylor who were in films I'd seen. And of course, Boris Karloff.

SCHWEITZER: What do you think is the best adaptation of anything of yours on film and why?

BLOCH: On film, I think the thing that came closest to doing what I had intended to do was *Asylum*. There were fewer changes in that. Usually it's a matter of doing a certain sequence in a picture the way one plans it. The first sequence of *Asylum* came off exactly as I wanted it to come off. The only trouble was that I'd written it for the third sequence, and they decided to switch it. I think they made a great mistake by putting it as the first sequence in that film, because it was so strong it overwhelmed what followed. I wanted to build up to that.

SCHWEITZER: If you care to mention it, what was the worst?

BLOCH: The worst was *The Deadly Bees*, I believe, which was a rewrite job done in England by somebody at the request of the director. The producers were away, and when they got back and saw the rewrite—they've said since—they were not happy with it. But everything in pre-production had been planned for it, and they didn't have the money to scrap all the pre-production sets, so they had to go ahead with it that way. That came off, I think, rather badly. This is no reflection on Anthony Marriot, the writer who took over my script there and did the rewrite. He did what he was told, and I'm sure he's a very competent man. But it didn't come off in the *slightest* as I had written it, because I had based it on a very fine book (H. F. Heard's *A Taste For Honey*). I had written the script with the book very much in mind, and it didn't bear any resemblance to it.

SCHWEITZER: Do you think this was because somebody thought it was commercially better?

BLOCH: I think that in some cases directors like to feel they have creative control. They believe in the *auteur* theory—that their judgment is better than the writer's—and they just do what they want, which is a human enough consideration.

SCHWEITZER: Have you ever thought of writing for the stage?

BLOCH: Yes. I would like very much to write for the stage in the abstract because I started out in amateur theatricals when I was a youngster, and did it all through high school. I wrote many skits; I used to sell gags to radio comedians. I did a little stand-up night club work in the Depression years, which nowadays is meaningless because you got ten dollars for an evening if you were fortunate enough to be employed. But, knowing what I do about the problems and pitfalls of theatrical production today, I don't think I'd have the stamina for it, because it's really, literally, an endless grind of rewriting and rewriting and rewriting. Even though a dramatist's words are protected by contract and nothing can be changed without his approval, he soon finds out that he better change or else—or else the play doesn't reach Broadway.

SCHWEITZER: You mean it's worse than television?

BLOCH: Much more so. Also, there's a very definite trend today towards kinkiness and freakiness and things to the left of Pinter and Ionesco which doesn't interest me. I don't like the idea of writing something that turns out to be an incoherent screaming match in which the audience is put down in four-letter words and every obscenity is dumped on them. To me this is not entertainment and it's not true theatre.

SCHWEITZER: Did you ever think about doing fantasy theatre? It seems to me that the stage is an ideal form for that because you can draw the audience into imagining things.

BLOCH: Well, here again there had been a tremendous economic problem. When I was not only a child, but a young man and a young adult as well, one went to the theatre expecting to see spectacle, and you got it. Many plays had four, five, six sets, and the musicals had lavish settings, tremendous casts. Today, the costs of production are such that most plays are confined to one set, two acts, and they prefer to have four or five actors, and that's it. Now, fantasy would require spectacle and illusion, and multiplicity of sets, which would not be achieved just by changing lights and costumes. The rock fantasy has prevailed simply because it can be done in that fashion, I think, but many times I'm struck by the fact that the young people who marvelled at something like *Hair* just didn't know about theatre in the past, because most of the things that were amusing in *Hair* were taken deliberately and directly from Olson and Johnson's *Hellzapoppin* in 1939. The gorilla climbing out in the audience, and all the other little schticks, were old vaudeville and revue material, and these were the things that impressed these kids who had never seen and didn't even know the names of those people.

SCHWEITZER: What I had in mind for fantasy was a production I saw of *Peer Gynt*, once, which was done virtually without props, in the round, and it worked beautifully.

BLOCH: Well, I don't like theatre in the round, and I don't like the "without props" thing and I don't like Shakespeare in modern dress or period costumes that are not Elizabethan. I think those things should be played straight. They're better than nothing, yeah, but if you have seen the authentic in the original, these substitutes suffer by comparison.

SCHWEITZER: Getting off that subject now—why were you drawn to writing horror stories?

BLOCH: Because I had the overactive imagination of a child, and a child's apprehension regarding death and the mysteries of existence. Also, I had seen Lon Chaney Sr. in his performances when I was a kid of seven or eight, and it scared the hell out of me. I developed the theory that if you can't lick 'em, join 'em, and I joined them.

SCHWEITZER: Do you think supernatural horror fiction appeals because it is filled with safe horrors? For instance we know there are no vampires.

BLOCH: Not only that, but you can control the horrors. You can evoke your vampire out of the grave, and at the end you can drive a stake through his heart and put him back. It is a way of handling evil. It is a way of handling dread, tragedy, and misfortune. You are in control of it—and I think this is the appeal to the audience too—that all of these creatures, monsters, and demons are at once safe and removed, whereas if there's a resemblance to natural disasters, or to recognizable human monsters, like murderers and psychopaths, there's a sick feeling, because it's a mirror up to nature...up to our own social order. You come away with a very queasy uneasiness.

SCHWEITZER: Why, then, do people read books like that? You've done several—things like *The Scarf*.

BLOCH: I think because, although no one has remarked on this fact, all of my books are morality plays in which virtue triumphs and evil does not get rewarded—as is the case in so many modern mainstream things in which the anti-hero rips off people and rapes and murders and indulges in far greater excesses than the villains, usually given the motivation of revenge, as if this justifies everything. We are living in an age in which there are series upon series of Executioners and Butchers and Killers, one-man vigilante teams that out-do Mickey Spillane, and I avoid that route. I think a lot of people would like the reassurance, the feeling that virtue does triumph and, while it's not popular to voice these sentiments, I think that if we all lose our faith in the triumph of goodness, then it's going to be anarchy, social chaos, nihilism. Why bother to be decent to everybody? Just go around and dump on everyone, and whatever you get away with is fine. It's the Watergate morality.

SCHWEITZER: It seems to me that when people go to see *Psycho*, they're more interested in watching the villain. Do you think this is because of a fascination with evil, and desire to get up close safely?

BLOCH: Well, in Freudian terms, the late Doctor Edmund Burgler did an examination among his patients as to how they felt about this kind of material and with whom they identified. I know about this because after I wrote *The Scarf*, he immediately queried me and asked me for my feelings on the subject, and then he told me what his observations were. He made a rather astute remark for a Freudian psychiatrist. He said that many of his patients who read this sort of material told him that they identified with the heroes, the policeman, the detective, or the hero that tries to solve the mystery. He said a much smaller percentage of the patients thought they were being very candid because they identified with the villain. They got rid of their aggressions and frustrations by rooting for him. But he said nobody gave him the answer which he thought was the basic one—the one which constitutes the primary feeling, and that is that many people unconsciously identified with the *victims*—that many of the latent paranoids in our society feel that there are forces conspiring against them, and they're looking for a devil theory—as witnessed by *The Exorcist* and *Rosemary's Baby* and similar things of that nature—and this is satisfying to them. They feel at one with the persecuted and maligned and tortured, while at the same time there is that satisfaction of knowing, in the end, justice is going to triumph. This is a reassurance that they don't find in real life.

SCHWEITZER: Do you think that Lovecraft works like that, with the persecuting forces represented by his shapeless unmentionables?

BLOCH: Absolutely. Again, he's invented his own mythos, his own cosmos in which the forces of good and evil do battle, and many of the evil events are explained by the fact that there are all-powerful, malignant, and mysterious entities who control our destinies. That relieves people of personal responsibility, and they aren't really responsible for pollution.

SCHWEITZER: But, strangely, evil always wins in those stories.

BLOCH: It always wins in those stories, and this is for the more pessimistic and cynical, I guess—a vindication of their attitudes. But what he is saying, in effect, and what they want to believe in, is: "Yes, evil does exist. There are such forces and that's the real reason behind all this. Don't you worry so much about mundane matters. You can't help it. You're in the grip of these terrors." He made it very convincing.

SCHWEITZER: So, how did you feel when you wrote stories like that?

BLOCH: Well, I started out, of course, as many writers did who were under his influence. By imitating Lovecraft, so naturally I used the plot structure and the form that he had. I didn't think about it consciously at the time. Later, I began to realize that many of the readers were intrigued by a twist or a surprise or a shock ending, so I just tried to give them what they wanted as entertainment. I found that this did entertain them, the people who read my work, and I consider myself primarily an entertainer. The morality aspect of it is a personal thing, but basically I'm always writing to entertain the portion of the audience reading or viewing that happens to dig this genre.

SCHWEITZER: Do you think that this sort of thing can mix effectively with humor?

BLOCH: Very much so, because humor and horror are two sides of the same coin. Both depend on the element of the grotesque and the unexpected, and much humor is horror when you analyze it. It deals with the misfortunes and tragedies of other people, handled in a humorous fashion. All the great comedians really are writing horror stories about the persecutions and afflictions of all the little men.

SCHWEITZER: It seems to me that the difference between horror and humor is that, in horror, the pain is there. In humor it is not. A black/white thing.

BLOCH: Unless you get into black humor, in which case the two are intermingled.

SCHWEITZER: In your story, "The Shadow from the Steeple," it seemed to me to be a little bit defused on the horror side because of the in-group references that came off as humor.

BLOCH: Well, I wrote it solely and expressly to round out as a trilogy the other two stories which were part of that: my "Shambler from the Stars," where I killed off Lovecraft, and his sequel, "The Haunter of the Dark," where he killed off me. I wanted to do a third story and sort of bring all those elements together. So, those references were deliberate and that was a sort of self-indulgence. I wasn't so much interested in bringing it off for an audience that wasn't familiar with the other two stories.

SCHWEITZER: When you were showing Lovecraft your manuscripts and he was criticizing them, did he encourage you to use his methods and, in effect, imitate him?

BLOCH: Not directly. He merely praised what I did, and if he made any criticisms, they were always couched as suggestions and largely were about factual matters. If I used his New England background he would say, "Now wait a minute, you have this happening in the wrong place," and he'd draw a little map and say, "Here's the geography of this particular town, and here is the history or genealogy of this reference that you make, and you might want to incorporate that." That was the extent of it.

SCHWEITZER: Didn't he somewhat revise one of your works?

BLOCH: That was a story called "Satan's Servants" (in *Something About Cats*). He sent me a map locating my imaginary town of Roodsford, and he made several of these genealogical and historical references in the form of footnotes, which I then incorporated into the story or referred to, but he did no actual rewriting of it whatsoever. So I had written it, and *Weird Tales* wasn't interested in it, so I put it away, and later Derleth said "Would you please let me print this?"

SCHWEITZER: Do you think that the fact that you did it yourself is the reason that, of all the people Lovecraft did any revision for at all, you're the only one who ever amounted to anything? For example, none of the heavy revision clients of his, that you see in *The Horror in the Museum*, ever sold anything by themselves or gained any reputation.

BLOCH: I think I was just lucky. I was fortunate to be able to break through into print on my own, so there might be an element of truth in what you say. I didn't lean on anyone as a crutch. Like I said earlier on about going out to Hollywood, I learned the hard way in the school of the Depression. You've got to do it on your own or else you'll have no inner security. If you have to rely on someone else, some exterior force, whether it's a person or a talisman or a compulsive ritual that you have to indulge in before you can write, you're really painting yourself into a corner. So I've tried to avoid these things.

SCHWEITZER: Why don't you write more science fiction than you have?

BLOCH: You're talking to someone who knows nothing whatsoever about the hard sciences, who was very deficient in mathematics and who, I think, has a psychological hang-up in as much as I like to be able to control the material that I work with. Therefore, I don't want to be bound by hard and fast scientific laws and premises and postulates. So much of the science fiction that I have done is science fiction by sufferance. It falls into that category because editors of science fiction magazines have been willing to accept it. But by-and-large, the closest approximation that you can make is if you call it scientific fantasy. It's just a matter of personal disinclination. You work from your strengths, and that's not one of my strengths.

SCHWEITZER: Sam Moskowitz once said that your writing of early science fiction helped draw you out of the Lovecraftian straightjacket, and got you to write dialogue and freer prose. Do you think this is so? Did science fiction widen the range of what you could do?

BLOCH: I think what happened was that I was dragooned into writing science fiction. I was a member of the Milwaukee Fictioneers, a writers' group which numbered among its membership Stanley G. Weinbaum, Raymond A. Palmer (who became the editor of *Amazing*), Ralph Milne Farley (Roger Sherman Hoar), and Arthur Tofte (who went into advertising, and is now retired and writing a whole slew of books for Roger Elwood and other people). But Ray Palmer, through the kind intercession of Roger Sherman Hoar (Farley), was appointed editor of *Amazing Stories* suddenly. He left our group in Milwaukee and went on to Chicago, and he had a lot of problems, because the magazine was going right down the tubes.
He looked over all the material that had been bought by his predecessor and it was terrible. So he immediately dashed back to Milwaukee, rounded up the Fictioneers, and said "You guys have gotta help me. I want each of you to write me a story." So I wrote my first science fiction story as a favor for Ray Palmer.

As the magazine got launched he said, "Write some more," so I did some more: "The Strange Flight of Richard Clayton," "The Man Who Walked Through Mirrors," and a couple of the other early ones—"Almost Human" and some of the others—were quite successful with his readership. Then I got onto this Lefty Feep business—humorous science fiction. I found that there was a greater market for humor in the science fiction field at that time than there was in the fantasy field, and I liked to write humor, so I just went on from there. I would say that it may very well have helped to broaden my writing, but I had already begun to change my style. I had departed from the Lovecraft thing in 1939 or 1940. It wasn't just in science fiction, because my fantasy was also changing style. I had been experimenting with writing style. I got into mystery and suspense because I admire the work of people like Raymond Chandler.

SCHWEITZER: How good of an editor do you think Palmer was? You may have heard the story about the Robert Moore Williams tale that was allegedly rejected for being "too good." It was "Robot's Return" and it sold to *Astounding*. Palmer supposedly said, "This is beautiful but it isn't pulp fiction." Did you find any such limitations?

BLOCH: No. I just wrote what I pleased for him. We never discussed anything in advance. I just sent the stories in, and as far as I know, he never rejected anything of mine over the years. I believe he was very conscious of the fact that his publishers, Ziff-Davis, were afraid of elevating their sights too high. He also felt, at that time, that *Astounding Science Fiction* was for the intellectuals and the highbrows and the MIT people, and he wasn't going to compete with them. He was going to go for a different audience, a more youthful audience, an audience of servicemen since this was the early 1940s—World War II time—and a little bit of a gaudier fantasy audience. It was a commercial consideration, but I can't ever recall him making a remark like that about any of the stories that anybody else had submitted.

SCHWEITZER: What editors do you think were most helpful to you?

BLOCH: Oddly enough, I've never had an editor in the fantasy or science fiction field who gave me many constructive suggestions for rewriting or changing, or who tossed ideas at me. The closest that has ever come was in the middle and late 1950s when editors were trying to put me on the spot by sending me a cover illustration, saying, "Here, you're going to write a story about this," and sometimes there was already a title on the cover. I did so, but that's about all the guidance I got. Most of the editors were helpful in the way Lovecraft was helpful—they encouraged me—but I never worked with an editor on rewriting, revising, restructuring, or restyling, largely because I never lived where the editors lived. Most of the markets were in New York, and I was in Milwaukee at the time. I occasionally went to Chicago to see Farnsworth Wright of *Weird Tales* and Palmer at *Amazing*, but those were social visits. I never had this promotional idea of going down and talking stories, and selling things over the luncheon table or over the bar, which probably was wrong, because that was the way in which people achieved status and got assignments—and they still do. But it wasn't my way. Again, I'm not putting it down, but it wasn't my particular thing.

SCHWEITZER: Did you ever have any dealing with John Campbell?

BLOCH: John and I didn't even meet until 1952. I had sold some material to *Unknown*, because it was a fantasy magazine, and I did it through an agency, and John never rejected anything. I felt the way Palmer felt, that John's *Astounding* was a quality science fiction magazine, which in that time—in the 1940s—was very much directed towards hard science and technology. I never submitted a story to John Campbell. But in 1952, I met John in Chicago, and we had an instant rapport. We were close friends from then on. I saw him at every convention—he and his wife Peg. At that time, Campbell was God. He was the deity who walked on Earth, and every time he came into a convention, he was surrounded by admirers and acolytes, and I was, for many years, toastmaster at those conventions. I made a point of getting up and insulting John, and just ripping him apart.

I married my present wife in 1964. She knew nothing about science fiction. She had never attended a convention and she didn't know these people. So, one time we were in London, and I was there to work on a film. A convention was happening there, so we were going to it. I was asked to speak, Arthur Clarke was the guest of honor, and John Campbell was there. So we walked into the hall before the banquet and Peg Campbell comes up to me and says, "Are you going to speak?" I said, "Yes, I'll speak." And she said, "Will you do me a favor? Will you please insult John? Because if you don't, he'll feel so hurt." And my wife did a double-take. She couldn't imagine this. So I got up there and, of course, that's exactly what I did. That was our relationship, and we never had a discussion about politics or regarding some of John's theories. I just didn't enter into it. It was a very personalized thing. He had a fine sense of humor and I so enjoyed being with him. For example, when a convention was out in Detroit, he took me and a few others out to the Ford Museum at Dearborn. We went through it and he knew everything about every artifact in the place, and to listen to this man discourse on that was a rare privilege.

SCHWEITZER: In what direction is your career going now?

BLOCH: Well, I took off some time to do some short stories, because I realized I hadn't done that for a long while. That's a labor of love. You can't earn a living in short stories. Then I'll probably return to television and films. I have three novels, two of which are contracted for, except that I won't sign the contracts because I don't want to be boxed in, and both of the publishers have said they're willing to wait until I do them. It's got to be the same old thing. Fifty-some-odd years in the business and I'm too old to learn new tricks. As Boris used to say when people would ask him about the Monster and what he was going to do now in his old age, he said, "I'm shameless. As long as they offer me work, I'm going to get up there and perform," and by God, this man did so with a brace on his leg, with one lung collapsed, when he was in his eighties. He was a magnificent man. I can't hope to measure up to him, but I admire his spirit and I understand it. He enjoyed, he had a love affair with his audience, and I think I always loved an audience too. I'm very grateful for what they've done for me all these years.

SCHWEITZER: Thank you, Mr. Bloch.

A SELECTED SECONDARY BIBLIOGRAPHY ON ROBERT BLOCH

Cave, Hugh B. "Robert Bloch: Writer and Gentleman," in *Weird Tales* 52 (Spring 1991): 50.

Collins, Tom. "Robert Bloch: Society as Insane Asylum," in *Twilight Zone* 1 (June 1981): 13-17.

Daniels, Les. Robert Bloch," in *Supernatural Fiction Writers*, edited by E. F. Bleiler. New York: Charles Scribner's Sons, 1985, p. 901-908.

Flanagan, Graeme. *Robert Bloch: A Bio-Bibliography*. Canberra City, Australia: Graeme Flanagan, 1979.

"In Pursuit of Pure Horror: Robert Bloch, Suzy McKee Charnas, Harlan Ellison, Gahan Wilson," in *Harper's* 279 (October 1989): 45-53.

Larson, Randall D. *The Complete Robert Bloch: An Illustrated International Bibliography*. Sunnyvale, CA: Fandom Unlimited Enterprises, 1986.

Larson, Randall D. "The Cthulhu Mythos Fiction of Robert Bloch," in *The Horror of It All*, edited by Robert M. Price. Mercer Island, WA: Starmond House, 1990, p. 71-74.

Larson, Randall D. "The Horror Fiction of Robert Bloch," in *Discovering Modern Horror Fiction II*, edited by Darrell Schweitzer. Mercer Island, WA: Starmont House, 1988.

Larson, Randall D. *Robert Bloch*. Mercer Island, WA: Starmont House, 1986.

Larson, Randall D. & Robert Bloch, eds. *The Robert Bloch Companion: Collected Interviews, 1969-86*. Mercer Island, WA: Starmont House, 1989.

Larson, Randall D. "Yours Truly, Robert Bloch," in *Discovering Modern Horror Fiction II*, edited by Darrell Schweitzer. Mercer Island, WA: Starmont House, 1988, p. 63-73.

Morrish, Bob. "*Weird Tales* Talks with Robert Bloch," in *Weird Tales* 52 (Spring 1991): 51-56.

Moskowitz, Sam. "'Psycho'-Logical Bloch," in *Amazing Stories* 36 (December 1962): 109- . Reprinted in: *Seekers of Tomorrow*, by Sam Moskowitz. Cleveland: World Publishing, 1966.

Price, Robert M. "Reconstructing the 'De Vermis Mysteriis,'" in *The Horror of It All*, edited by Robert M. Price. Mercer Island, WA: Starmond House, 1990, p. 75-79.

Punter, David. "Robert Bloch's *Psycho*: Some Pathological Contexts," by *American Horror Fiction: From Brockden Brown to Stephen King*, edited by Brian Docherty. New York: St. Martin's Press, 1990, p. 92-106.

"Robert Bloch," in *Contemporary Literary Criticism, Volume 33*. Detroit: Gale Research Co., 1985, p. 82-86.

Robert Bloch Bibliography. Tewkesbury, Gloucester: [s.n.], 1965.

Sinor, Bradley H. "*Weird Tales* Talks Again with Robert Bloch," in *Weird Tales* 52 (Spring 1991): 89-92.

Stableford, Brian. "The Short Fiction of Robert Bloch," in *Survey of Modern Fantasy Literature*, edited by Frank N. Magill. Englewood Cliffs, NJ: Salem Press, 1983, Vol. 3, p. 1452-1456.

Wiater, Stanley. "Bloch of Prose," in *Fear* no. 13 (January 1990): 9-11.

Wiater, Stanley. "Robert Bloch," in *Dark Dreamers: Conversations with the Masters of Horror*. New York: Avon, 1990, p. 19-26.

Winter, Douglas E. "Robert Bloch," in *Faces of Fear*. New York: Berkley Books, 1985, p. 10-22.

II.

RAMSEY CAMPBELL

A RAMSEY CAMPBELL CHRONOLOGY

1946   John Ramsey Campbell born January 4, at Liverpool, England.

1951-53 Educated at Christ the King Primary School, Liverpool.

1953-57 Educated at Ryebank Private School, Liverpool.

1957-62 Attends Saint Edward's College, Liverpool.

1958   Campbell submits an illustrated book-length collection of stories to T. V. Boardman & Co., and gets an encouraging rejection letter.

1962   First professional publication, "The Church in High Street," in *Dark Mind, Dark Heart* edited by August Derleth (Arkham House).

1962-66 Works as a tax officer.

1964   *The Inhabitant of the Lake and Less Welcome Tenants* (collection) published by Arkham House.

1966-73 Works as a library assistant.

1969   Begins reviewing films for BBC Radio Merseyside (to present).

1971   Marries Jenny Chandler, daughter of science-fiction writer A. Bertram Chandler, January 1.

1973   Becomes a full-time writer; *Demons by Daylight* (collection) published by Arkham House.

1976   *The Doll Who Ate His Mother: A Novel of Modern Terror* published by Bobbs-Merrill; *The Height of the Scream* (collection) published by Arkham House; *Superhorror* (anthology) published by W. H. Allen (UK, republished as *The Far Reaches of Fear*, Allen, 1980).

1977   *The Doll Who Ate His Mother*, "The Companion," *Height of the Scream*, and *Superhorror* nominated for World Fantasy Awards; novelizations of classic films, *The Bride of Frankenstein*, *The Wolfman*, and *Dracula's Daughter* (republished as by E. K. LEYTON, 1980), are published by Berkley Books under the house pseudonym of CARL DREADSTONE.

1978   "The Chimney" wins World Fantasy Award, Best Short Story; "Loveman's Comeback" nominated for World Fantasy Award; "In the Bag" wins British Fantasy Award, Best Short Story.

1979   Daughter, Tammy Joanne, born, August; *The Face That Must Die* published by Star Books (UK).

1980   *The Parasite* (British title: *To Wake the Dead*, Millington) published by Macmillan; *New Tales of the Cthulhu Mythos* (anthology) published by Arkham House; *New Terrors* (2 vol. anthology) published by Pan (UK & Australia, the 1 vol. ed. published by Pocket Books in 1984 is significantly abridged); *The Parasite* wins British Fantasy Award, Best Novel; "Mackintosh Willy" wins World Fantasy Award, Best Short Story.

1981   Son, Matt Ramsey, born, June; *New Terrors 1* nominated for World Fantasy Award; *The Nameless* published by Macmillan (UK); *Through the Walls* published by the British Fantasy Society.

1982   *Dark Companions* (collection) published by Fontana/Collins.

1983   *Incarnate* published by Macmillan; *The Claw* published by Macmillan under the pseudonym JAY RAMSEY (published under Campbell's own name as *Night of the Claw* by Tor, 1985); revised edition of *The Face That Must Die* published by Scream/Press; *The Gruesome Book* (anthology for young readers) published by Piccolo & Pan Books (UK & Australia).

1984   *Watch the Birdie* published by Rosemary Pardoe.

1985   *Obsessions* published by Granada; *Incarnate* wins British Fantasy Award, Best Novel; *Cold Print* published by Scream/Press; revised edition of *The Nameless* published by Panther (UK); *Slow* published by Footsteps Press.

1986   *The Hungry Moon* published by Macmillan; *Night Visions 3* (anthology with Clive Barker and Lisa Tuttle) and *Black Wine*, (anthology with Charles L. Grant, edited by Douglas Winter), published by Dark Harvest; *The Tomb Herd and Others* (collection of early, previously uncollected Cthulhu Mythos stories) published as special issue of *Crypt of Cthulhu* no. 43, Hallowmas.

1987   *Dark Feasts: The World of Ramsey Campbell* (collection) published by Robinson (UK); *Scared Stiff: Tales of Sex and Death* (collection) published by Scream/Press; *Ghostly Tales* published as special issue of *Crypt of Cthulhu* no. 50, Michaelmas (juvenilia, see 1958); *Cold Print* republished by Tor; *The Doll Who Ate His Mother*, expanded edition, published by Century (UK); *Medusa* published by Footsteps Press.

1988   *The Influence* published by Macmillan; *Fine Frights: Stories That Scared Me* (collection) published by Tor; *The Hungry Moon* wins British Fantasy Award, Best Novel; *Scared Stiff* nominated for World Fantasy Award.

1989   *Ancient Images* published by Legend Century (UK) and Tor; *The Influence* wins British Fantasy Award, Best Novel.

1990   *Needing Ghosts* (novella) published by Legend (UK); *Midnight Sun* published by Macdonald (UK) & Tor; *Best New Horror* (anthology, co-edited with Stephen Jones) published by Robinson (UK).

1991   *The Count of Eleven* published by Macdonald (UK); *Midnight Sun* and *Waking Nightmares* (collection) published by Tor; *Uncanny Banquet* (anthology) published; *The Best New Horror* wins World Fantasy Award, Best Anthology; Ramsey Campbell issue of *Weird Tales* appears, Summer; *Best New Horror 2* (anthology with Stephen Jones) published by Robinson (UK).

1992   *The Count of Eleven* published by Tor; *Uncanny Banquet* (anthology) published by Little, Brown (UK).

1993   *Alone With the Horrors* (a thirty-year retrospective collection) published by Arkham House; *The Long Lost* published by Headline (UK); *Strange Things and Stranger Places* (collection) published by Tor; *Deathport* (anthology) published by Pocket Books.

A RAMSEY CAMPBELL INTERVIEW

SCHWEITZER: You seem to have disowned the Cthulhu Mythos in your writing. You signed a copy of *Demons by Daylight* for me as "my first good book." Why is this?

CAMPBELL: I think it's because I regard *The Inhabitant of the Lake* as a kind of youthful indiscretion—something I had to do, but which is now over. We have to go right back to the beginning, I suppose, and say how I wrote *The Inhabitant of the Lake*. It was partly because I had read all of *Cry Horror!* in one day, and that was the first big jolt of Lovecraft I'd ever had. And, having written a great many stories before which were unpublishable, I realized that here was something I could do which might actually satisfy me, that would let me say to myself, "My God! This reads exactly like Lovecraft because it says things like 'eldritch' and 'amorphous' and 'nameless' and 'shoggoths' and stuff like this." So I wrote those stories and sent them to August Derleth. They were all set in Arkham country, originally, so you had amazingly unconvincing American rustics mumbling in sort of curious half-English accents. I rewrote that, and I was stuck in the groove, for a while, of imitating Lovecraft, which indeed I did, and when I began to develop my own style in a few stories you won't see very often—except one called "Before the Storm"—I was still leaning very heavily on this Lovecraftian crutch.

What happened later is that I was reacting against this sort of thing, not against what Lovecraft had done, but quite the contrary, against what I had done to Lovecraft. Which is to say, the Cthulhu Mythos was intended to imply a lot more than it actually states, and that was the whole idea of it. Lovecraft didn't conceive of it as an entity anyway, only as a series of glimpses of something much larger. Here I came along and—with all due respect to him because he's a friend of mine—so had Brian Lumley and some of the others, and we said, "Here are all these loose ends and we're going to tie it up into a nice neat package so you can see exactly who is whose half-brother and who is whose minion and all that." And it seemed to me that it was *ruining* exactly what Lovecraft was trying to do. So I went rushing off in the other direction. I wrote some of the stories in *Demons by Daylight* in a body. I had a period in which I wrote just a few stories which were not very good and they were sort of *hesitating* really. One or two got published, like "The Stone on the Island," which you can still see as transitional. Then, all of a sudden, I had this burst of the *Demons by Daylight* stuff. It was all very enigmatic. It is, in fact, a violent reaction against what I was doing. Instead of explaining everything, I wasn't explaining anything at all. You've got stuff like "The End of Summer's Day," which is *totally* enigmatic. I mean *I* can't explain it to you any more than anyone else can explain it to me. I quite like those stories, though. I do think that they do work in a very curious way in a sense of meaning themselves and not being accessible to explanation. Of course, I had to get beyond that, too, and write stories that were more coherent.

SCHWEITZER: Did you realize from the start that you would have to get beyond rewriting Lovecraft, or did this come as a realization later on?

CAMPBELL: Oh, much later on. There were a few odd things, like the first draft of "The Interloper," by my good friend Errol Undercliffe, which was a lot more heavily Lovecraftian. I began very tentatively, as if saying, "Well, *maybe* I don't have to refer to Cthulhu in this story if it's not about the Lovecraftian deities. Maybe I can leave that out. Maybe I actually don't have to preface the story with a quotation from the *Necronomicon.*" So it was a very gradual process of moving away, and once I found where I was going I think I began to develop *intuitively*, if I can say that with any kind of coherence.

SCHWEITZER: Do you think you could go back now and do a Mythos story in a totally different way, rather than imitate?

CAMPBELL: Well, I actually did have a go. I did a story called "The Voice of the Beach." I'll tell you what I was trying to do there. I got very worried when, in England, I asked an audience how many of them had read Lovecraft, and all the hands went up. Okay, how many had read Blackwood? And three-quarters of the hands stayed down. There seems to be this extraordinary lack of knowledge of the tradition in which Lovecraft was working. So I decided I wanted to go back to the roots of the Cthulhu Mythos—which I take to be Lovecraft attempting to equal Blackwood's "The Willows," and certain stories by Machen—purely because this is what Lovecraft admired most of all in the genre. He was trying to get back to that, and the interesting thing is that he doesn't quite achieve it in any of his stories, but he achieves something quite different that he's not quite aiming at. He goes off in a different direction. But I wanted to try and get back to this attempt to write stories which didn't so much explain things directly as put together a series of glimpses of something very large and very awesome and ominous, without leaning very heavily on the Lovecraftian thing. Actually, the only thing I really did with that story was I put in some fairly typical Lovecraftian language, this thing about a chanting which is heard in various and increasingly bizarre ways. But *really* it was an attempt to do for a beach scene—a sort of Salvador Dali beach if you like—what Blackwood does for willows on the Danube and Lovecraft does for the hills of New England. I don't know how successful it is. Lin Carter looked at it once. Maybe I'll have a chance to find out people's opinions sometime soon.

SCHWEITZER: Do you think the Cthulhu Mythos as it exists now is worked out? For instance, it strikes me that Bob Bloch's *Strange Eons* is a book-length mercy killing.

CAMPBELL: [*laughs*] Yes, I think you could say that. But it's a very affectionate one. I mean, it's putting the poor old sop out of its misery, really. Yes, I think the whole thing has become awfully overpopulated—not to say overwritten and undercharacterized. Mind you, I think my Arkham anthology shows there are still worthwhile ways of developing the Mythos, especially by being true to yourself rather than imitating Lovecraft. But in general, it's just become an absurd sort of proliferation. I can't think of a good example. I'll tell you what it reminds me of. It's like a modern city that started as a nice little settlement and now seems to grow up with concrete estates without anybody doing anything about them.

SCHWEITZER: What do you see as a more fruitful direction to be explored?

CAMPBELL: Well, where I'll put my money as a writer—Peter Timlett had a word for it; he called it the "humanist tale of terror," which is a good vague term which I need to explain. What he had in mind was the tale of the supernatural which is very closely related to the psychology of the protagonist, whoever it might be. The important thing, as far as I'm concerned, is that I tend to write more stories where the supernatural element does relate very directly to something in the victim's psychology. More often than not, it's a childhood fear or a childhood trauma that was apparently dealt with, but was really repressed, and pops up in a much worse form. But the important thing, I think, is that in these stories you can't just explain it away. You can't use the psychology to explain the supernatural and say, "*That* is what it's all about." Equally, the supernatural in these stories has got to have a distinct power of its own. It can't just be a symbol of whatever is within the victim. I find this an interesting avenue to explore. Mind you, this is strictly personal, or at least it's particularly personal for me. When I was writing in the Lovecraft vein, I was really writing somebody else's fiction. I was doing a gloss on Lovecraft. But the more I write now the closer I get to writing about my own fears. My recent stuff has mostly been a kind of journey into things in my early life which I preferred to forget about or not look at too closely. For example, I was, until my early teens, terrified of the dark the way the character in the story "The Companion" is. It's only very recently that I remembered I had been like that until I was about fourteen or fifteen. So these stories are almost a process of self-discovery. I hope they're more than that, though.

SCHWEITZER: Is it always necessary for the protagonist of such a story to be the victim?

CAMPBELL: No, I don't think it so, necessarily, and you're going to ask me to prove that, aren't you? You're going to ask me to think of a good example. I don't know. Maybe it is to me. I seem to write about victims, but not passive victims. I think that's the important distinction. There is the horror story in which the protagonist will just sit there at the mercy of the plot, at the mercy of the supernatural. I don't particularly want to write that, except very occasionally. I suppose the stories are not so much about the struggle between good and evil any more—or not mine anyway—but more about the struggle with something that is within the character as much as not. So we're not talking about victims any more. We're talking about the characters coming to terms with themselves. I did have a run of stories where this pessimism became an almost automatic thing, so you *knew* at the end of the story the worst is inevitably going to happen. I got rather tired of this. I also thought it was a bit too easy. I wasn't attempting to explore the story properly. So I did have a few stories over the past several years in which the character fights his or her way out, but only at the cost of extreme psychic pain.

SCHWEITZER: Do you ever have the problem of your characters coming to accept what is going on as supernatural too quickly for it to be plausible? We as readers, because the story is in *Frights* or *Whispers*, or some such place, *know* that it's a supernatural story and therefore the supernatural explanation of the strange happenings is the correct one. But, in the real world, a sane person has to eliminate every other possibility first. If he goes through the whole process in the story, because we know what's really going on, the story seems overlong and belaboring the obvious. What do you do about that?

CAMPBELL: I think it's more a case of stylistic indirection or having the character say, "This has got to so-and-so," at the same time the reader knows it is nothing of the kind. It's not that difficult to do. M. R. James used to have a wonderful line in this sort of thing. As you know, all his stories were about three thousand words long, and yet he used to pack in exactly this sort of thing you're talking about. He would do it in an extremely terse way. You would just have somebody look out of the window and see something like a seagull's wing, a white wing and the character saying, "Oh, that's just a seagull's wing," but the reader knows damned well it's nothing of the kind. I think you can play that game with the reader. We are slightly ahead of the character, and I hope that, in the best stories, the development is also slightly ahead of the reader.

SCHWEITZER: Lovecraft's "At the Mountains of Madness" strikes me as an appalling botch in this area. After they've dissected these things which have remained preserved for millions of years—and then the specimens disappear, and there are footprints everywhere—still the characters refuse to believe that there might be one of them alive.

CAMPBELL: That's right. You mustn't let your characters do that kind of thing. Lovecraft said himself he wasn't interested in character. I think the single most important thing in this kind of fiction is believable motivation. The one thing I can't stand is the character who walks into the room from which we have been hearing noises, for no better reason than that the plot requires him to go to the other side of the door. If there isn't a better way of getting him in there than that, then forget it! The other rather peculiar thing is that I tended to feel, for a long time, that you had to take it as Lovecraft generally did, step by step, and really keep to the very last moment the revelation that it is the supernatural after all. As you say...belabor the point through every single possibility that it is not. Today, many of us would tend to say, "Oh yes, it *is* the supernatural" at a fairly early stage in the proceedings, largely because the occult seems to be rather fashionably acceptable now. It's something you can believe in without coming very much to terms with it. So, in many stories you do get people accepting very early on that there can be a haunted house. I had a problem, which is a slightly different problem, with a novel called *To Wake the Dead*, which is, among other things, fundamentally about a lady who finds herself developing inadvertent astral projection. Fairly early on in that, I thought I had to say to the reader that this is not a dream; it's real. You have to do it slightly before the character believes it. When the reader is in there all right, the character is still going to the psychiatrist and hoping for the best.

SCHWEITZER: What's wrong with so many Cthulhu Mythos stories is that they spend the entire story reaching this point. The archetypical last line is, *The monsters were real!* It seems to me that the thing to do is play the *Dracula* game by establishing early that it's real, but you don't establish all that it can do. If you wrote *Dracula* in a classic Mythos manner, it would build up to, "My God! He was a vampire!" and that would be the end of it.

CAMPBELL: That's right. It's a short story method to a large extent. You can't make that work with a novel particularly, and this is where I think Lovecraft did fall down with "At the Mountains of Madness." On the other hand, you look at *The Case of Charles Dexter Ward*, which I think is one of the great structures in horror fiction. That's one worth studying.

SCHWEITZER: That was one of the few cases where he actually seemed to understand novel structure. But then he went back to writing over-long short stories later and he never submitted that one anywhere. Do you think the supernatural form is more suited for short stories than novels?

CAMPBELL: Well, I used to feel—largely because I wrote them for thirteen years without doing anything else—that must be the best way. But I think there's a difference with the novel, really. It's a question of finding sufficient psychological plot so you don't have to throw in all your supernatural material early on. You sometimes start off with some sort of revelation, too. There was, for a long, long time, the myth that the supernatural horror novel was an extremely difficult thing to write, or at least to do with any kind of success. When you get to thinking about it, you realize that there are people as different as Walter de la Mare and, recently, Stephen King, Peter Straub, and others, who have done it. Then it becomes apparent that what was really wrong, probably, was this assumption by so many people that it wasn't worth trying in the first place. I'm inclined to feel now that the novel is a very strong structure if you can get it right, particularly because you have enormous opportunity for a long, slow, inexorable buildup.

SCHWEITZER: I think the reason people would believe this is because they would look at the significant supernatural fiction of Machen and James and Blackwood and see that it was all short stories. You can't maintain a straight atmosphere of terror all the way through a four hundred-page book. It has to be orchestrated and given its ups and downs.

CAMPBELL: With enormous care, yes indeed.

SCHWEITZER: How much can you mix completely different tones without wrecking the result, like mixing horror and humor?

CAMPBELL: There used to be a trend in horror movies, particularly the Hammer kind, where you wrote in a little scene with a comic porter who fell down or came in and saw the monster and fell over backwards in a comic fit. I don't think that sort of thing really works, but I do think that there are very strong elements of comedy in much horror fiction anyway, a strong element of black humor. I'm inclined to feel that we ought to be alive to writing this, in the sense of not blocking it out. There is a tendency to go through enormous contortions to avoid any possible absurdity. I think it's really a question of quite the opposite, of risking absurdity in the horror story. Now I remember...Ah! I can probably visit you on this and you've forgotten all about it. You reviewed "The Chimney" and you didn't know how much of it was meant to be funny. I don't think that matters. I think that, in a sense, if you found it a funny story, that's fine. I don't think that matters at all. Where horror and humor meet tends to be in the grotesque, and that's such a thin dividing line that I think it's impossible for any writer to control which side of that the reader is going to come down on.

SCHWEITZER: Particularly in your story "Heading Home." This struck me as an amazingly audacious piece, as if you were gleefully dancing on the grave of all the rules for this sort of story, particularly in the viewpoint shift, which is what some editors call a "tomato surprise." That is, lying about the basic facts until the end. But somehow this one worked.

CAMPBELL: Yeah, I thought that was fun. I was really playing around with the old EC horror comics. I was revisiting my misspent...well, it wasn't my misspent youth because I only got to read the EC's very recently. They were banned in Britain before I ever got around to them. Well, as I say...this whole thing about horror and humor: it just seems to me that there are so many similarities between the two forms. Both tend to deal in palatable and acceptable terms—in the sense of setting up within some kind of fiction—taboos and things people don't want to think about too clearly, like death, or the very things that humor does deal with. Also, the single most important thing in both horror and humor is timing. If you haven't got it, then I think you're never really going to write a good horror story. It probably can be learned. You study the masters. I suppose I tended to learn it from Robert Bloch, particularly the timing of certain of his effects, and from James—M. R. James rather than Henry—perhaps above all, the mastery of just the glancing reference that takes you when you aren't quite expecting it: the leather bag that slips out of the alcove and puts its arms around you, which is probably my favorite of all images of the kind. Or more recently in Stephen King's *The Shining*—well, I'm not going to ruin it for anyone who hasn't read it—but the thing that happens when the little boy goes into the hotel room with the bath, and the way the final effect of that chapter is timed. That is absolutely crucial in this field. At the same time there are writers who just don't have it. It's an awful book anyway, but the single worst example of mistiming I can think of is in *The Amityville Horror*. But then that's a piece of junk anyway. It's hardly worth talking about.

SCHWEITZER: The difference I see between humor and horror is that both deal with a grotesque situation, but in humor it doesn't hurt. For instance, if you hit somebody on the head with a hammer, it can be a bloody murder scene, or you can get a bonking on wood and it's a Three Stooges routine.

CAMPBELL: Although now, the grotesque in humor is getting more and more prevalent. In *Monty Python*, people *do* get bitten in the throat by carnivorous rabbits and bleed all over the place. Or going back to the Blake Edwards comedies with Peter Sellers. When Herbert Lom put his finger in the cigar-cutter by mistake, you knew he actually was going to chop it off, even if you didn't see it. So humor is getting steadily blacker. This is one of the many reasons for its popularity. The great example has got to be Bob Bloch, where some of the humor is so close to horror that it's practically impossible to tell the difference. If you were to make two piles, one of Bob's horror stories, one of his humor stories, you're going to have a hell of a lot left in the middle.

SCHWEITZER: Something like "The Closer of the Way."

CAMPBELL: That's right. What is that? It's autobiographical, with humor anyway.

SCHWEITZER: It's a giant in-joke, but...

CAMPBELL: Yes, but a very bizarre one for all that.

SCHWEITZER: This is, after all, the guy who has the heart of a little boy on his desk.

CAMPBELL: That's right.

SCHWEITZER: Still, what could be horror in these cases isn't done realistically. In Monty Python's dismembering of the black knight, it looks like they got a little garden hose...

CAMPBELL: Sure enough. But then a lot of horror isn't realistic either. There tends to be grotesque exaggeration, but it comes at it from the other direction, I suppose.

SCHWEITZER: Do you think you could write a book-length horror comedy?

CAMPBELL: I don't know. I wouldn't mind trying sometime. I used to do comedy scripts for the BBC for a little while, which tended awfully close. In fact, one of the producers was always saying, "Look, this is a bit heavy. It's a bit grim. Can't you lighten this up a bit?" Which is probably one reason why the show didn't last very long.

SCHWEITZER: One example I've seen which really astonished me was John Bellairs' *The Face in the Frost*, which jumps from horror to comedy in a couple of pages and back again and the mood is absolute in each section. It even contains a Lovecraft joke, which brings us back to the Cthulhu Mythos. It's used a lot for humor these days.

CAMPBELL: Well, it always was an in-joke to some extent, with Klarkash Ton and the Comte d'Erlette and so forth. Who is this guy Lumley invented? Therled Gustau, isn't it? Derleth backwards.

SCHWEITZER: To change the subject, was your early development influenced by the various other early writers?

CAMPBELL: Oh, yes. Particularly M. R. James. He was my great idol from a very early age, particularly because he took the comfortable English ghost story and made it nasty in an extreme surrealist way, where things turned up in places where they shouldn't be and really couldn't be. Where you would put your hand under a pillow and put it in a mouth. The finest of the whole lot is "Oh Whistle and I'll Come to You," where he takes the terrible old cliché of the ghost with the sheet over its head—you know, it's just so dull—and the trouble with that one is there's nobody inside it when you get up to look at it close. So he had an enormous influence. He has this extreme facility with just the turn of phrase that's frightening, whereas Lovecraft, given all my admiration for him, would tend to take a paragraph to get an effect. James is more likely to get it with three words and tag it on at the end of a sentence. Fritz Leiber, in his urban stories, is an enormous influence. I love those things; "Smoke Ghost" particularly. I thought I wouldn't mind writing something like that when I read it, and I think that's where I began to do urban horror stories.

SCHWEITZER: You mention the comfortable English ghost story. It seems to me that when it's comfortable, it's not working.

CAMPBELL: Absolutely. That's what I meant, really. There was a lot of that stuff around. But Le Fanu isn't comfortable. Actually the strangest example, to come back to that humor thing for a moment, of trying to find the dividing line, is L. P. Hartley in things like "The Travelling Grave." It's a most extraordinary story—not to give you too much of the plot—about a country house party where the *pièce de résistance* is a coffin which will swallow anybody who happens to be around, then burrow under the floorboards with them. It is never explained very completely why this thing happens to be around at all. And then the payoff is that one of the party disappears and they find a shoe upside-down on the floor. When they try and tug on it, they find the foot is still in it and they can't get it out of the floor. It's impossible to say which side of that dividing line we're on. We seem to be reeling drunkenly back and forth over it, I think. But no, the comfortable ghost stories I would associate with are—not Cynthia Asquith in her early days; she was very good then—those *Ghost Book* anthologies later on did tend to get a bit moribund. It was the same old gimmicks, the phantom dog, the person who said "Do you believe in ghosts?" "No." Then they disappear. All this sort of rather tired stuff.

SCHWEITZER: Well, she only edited the first three of those books.

CAMPBELL: That's right. Yes. It was when she left that they started to go downhill. There was still the occasional Aickman story there to light up the surrounding morass.

SCHWEITZER: The "Do you believe in ghosts?" gimmick has to be inherently comic. Do you know Dunsany's "In a Dim Room?"

CAMPBELL: Yes. You're talking about the progenitor there, probably; but for the umpteenth time it gets a little tiring.

SCHWEITZER: Are you satisfied with what's being written in the field today?

CAMPBELL: I'm pretty happy with quite a lot of it. You run down the list with people like Stephen King, Peter Straub, and Fritz Leiber. There are some very interesting people on the way up, I think. You see, I edited a big anthology for Pan Books in England. It's a quarter of a million words and I managed to get in quite a few new people. There's a brilliant guy named Marc Laidlaw, who was, I suppose, nineteen when his first story was published. He struck me as being a much better writer at that age than I was. He also is enormously professional. He'll rewrite till the cows come home if you want him to do it. He seems to me to be extraordinarily good.

SCHWEITZER: He's published a little bit in this country, too.

CAMPBELL: Ah, good. Fine. Well, look out for him, because he's going to be a big one, I think. Then in quite a different tradition is someone like Kathleen Resch, who started with one poem in an Andy Offutt anthology. I bought a 25,000 worder from her, which is a vampire story, but done with enormous intensity and freshness which made it irresistible to me. So, I'm delighted to see that there does seem to be another generation of writers in this field who are going to be very good. Actually I think that now that horror fiction does get up onto the bestseller list, the good people who used to be sitting around doing other work begin to come out again.

SCHWEITZER: It looked for a while as if the whole field was going under.

CAMPBELL: I think that was partly because the majority of good things in the field, despite that fact that novels can be done, are short stories, and there wasn't really that much of a market. The anthology was dead for awhile, but now all of a sudden you've got Charlie Grant and Stuart Schiff and Kirby McCauley. They have all revitalized the field. But it looked bad there for a while, I agree.

SCHWEITZER: What if you had come along ten years earlier and there wasn't much of a market? Would you have continued to write like you do?

CAMPBELL: I might have continued to write like I do anyway, because for a long while I wasn't selling a great deal. For quite a while I was putting things aside and saying, "Okay, with enough of these I can do another Arkham House book," which was *Demons by Daylight*. But I didn't take much time to try to sell those stories. There weren't many people around buying except for Bob Lowndes. There weren't enough to make a living at it. I could just do those stories for my own satisfaction, or my own relative satisfaction. But, inevitably, if it had come to the pinch...but then on the other hand, if I hadn't been selling reasonably well I couldn't have thought of going freelance full time. I suppose I would have given up writing except for the occasional story and not gone freelance at all.

SCHWEITZER: Would you have gone into mystery-suspense? A publisher tried to market one of your books that way, anyway.

CAMPBELL: [*snarls*] Don't tell me that. I *know* that. My *God!* They took out ads in *Ellery Queen*'s for *The Doll Who Ate His Mother* and a year later people at conventions were coming up to me saying, "When is that going to be published?" They hadn't seen any ads. But no, I don't think I could. Something like *The Doll* shades over toward the suspense story, to the extent the scene in the cellar was almost a kind of tribute to Bob Bloch and his cellar scene in *Psycho*. That whole scene of going through the house. The one attempt I have made at writing a psychological thriller with no supernatural elements is *The Face That Must Die*, which was published first in England, but which seems to me to be my poorest work. So I don't think I would survive very long in that field. `

SCHWEITZER: Is this because you don't feel inclined to write suspense?

CAMPBELL: Yes. I don't think I get good plots that way. The plots come out of the air and they tend to be nearly all at least fantastic in some form. Supernatural terror usually. If somebody comes along and says, "Look, I'm doing an anthology about so-and-so," I can usually work around and see if I can't come up with a new, say, demonic possession story. I did one for Michel Parry a while ago. More usually, it will be that the plot comes out of the back of my brain one morning and has to be written, because I'm more of a compulsive writer than a writer to order. It's a question of getting all these things down on paper, because I feel very edgy if I don't write for any length of time. If I'm away from work, I tend to get rather on edge. So it's a compulsion and not so much a case of my saying, "Okay, next I'm going to write a western," or whatever it might be. It's just that nearly all the stories that are in there waiting to be written are in the genre. The time I tried to do science fiction, for example, it had some really pretty embarrassing results. Luckily only one of those stories got published.

SCHWEITZER: What are your actual writing methods like?

CAMPBELL: Painful. No, they're not any more. What I do is that every morning when I'm writing a story, I go to my desk at about eight o'clock or maybe a little bit earlier. At that stage I am running the first paragraph that I'm going to write through my mind. I'm working out what that will be, because if I sit down and don't know what the paragraph is going to be, I just sit there and stare out of the window at the backyard and the cats walking along the alley wall. So I have to know what the first paragraph is going to be. I usually go through then to early afternoon, with luck. Occasionally, I go much later and write quite a large chunk, a chapter or something, depending on if it's going very well. The one problem that I have, or I used to have before I got over it, is that I review films for the BBC. I'd go off to press shows of them in the morning about ten o'clock and that means I just get the two hours in the morning to write. I figured out that as long as I know what the next paragraph is going to be, I can note it down in the notebook, then come back in the afternoon after the film and go on. I do. I do that every day while I am writing a story. That's the first draft. Then I type it and that involves chopping large chunks out. Maybe that's the version that gets published, or maybe that's the version the editor asks to be revised.

SCHWEITZER: Do you work from outlines?

CAMPBELL: Yes. Very heavily. I have a notebook always with me, and I note down any number of fragments for any given story that I'm writing. Then I'll mark those with a colored pen the night before I write. I mark up the things in those notes that I hope to use the following day in the scene I hope to complete. With a novel, of course, it's a question of making a whole notebook out of chapter outlines and another notebook which indexes those chapter outlines, and another book which indexes something else. So I'm surrounded by notebooks and lots of colored pens, and the whole thing is usually comprehensible to me, but not to anybody else.

SCHWEITZER: Thank you, Mr. Campbell.

A SELECT SECONDARY BIBLIOGRAPHY ON RAMSEY CAMPBELL

Ashley, Mike, ed. *Fantasy Reader's Guide to Ramsey Campbell*. Wallsend, Tyne & Wear, England: Cosmos Literary Agency, 1980.

Barker, Clive. "Ramsey Campbell: An Appreciation," in *Clive Barker's Shadows of Eden*, edited by Stephen Jones. Novato, CA, Lancaster, PA: Underwood-Miller, 1991, p. 83-88.

Brosnan, John. "Terror Tactics," in *Clive Barker's Shadows of Eden*, edited by Stephen Jones. Novato, CA, Lancaster, PA: Underwood-Miller, 1991, p. 89-94.

Crawford, Gary William. *"The Parasite,"* in *Survey of Modern Fantasy Literature,* edited by Frank N. Magill. Englewood Cliffs, NJ: Salem Press, 1983, Vol. 3, p. 1209-1211.

Crawford, Gary William. *Ramsey Campbell.* Mercer Island, WA: Starmont House, 1988.

Crawford, Gary William. "The Short Fiction of Ramsey Campbell," in *Survey of Modern Fantasy Literature,* edited by Frank N. Magill. Englewood Cliffs, NJ: Salem Press, 1983, Vol. 3, p. 1485-1488.

Crawford, Gary William. "Urban Gothic: The Fiction of Ramsey Campbell," in *Discovering Modern Horror Fiction,* edited by Darrell Schweitzer. Mercer Island, WA: Starmont House, 1985, p. 13-20.

Joshi, S. T., editor. *The Count at Thirty: A Tribute to Ramsey Campbell.* Necronomicon Press, 1993.

Jurkiewicz, Kenneth. "Ramsey Campbell," in *Supernatural Fiction Writers,* edited by E. F. Bleiler. New York: Charles Scribner's Sons, 1985, p. 993-1000.

Klein, T. E. D. "Ramsey Campbell: An Appreciation," in *Nyctalops* no. 13 (1977). Reprinted: *Discovering Modern Horror Fiction II,* edited by Darrell Schweitzer. Mercer Island, WA: Starmont House, 1988, p. 88-102.

Lane, Joel. "Negatives in Print: The Novels of Ramsey Campbell," in *Foundation* no. 36 (Summer 1986): 35-45.

Morrison, Michael A. "The Form of Things Unknown: Metaphysical and Domestic Horror in Ramsey Campbell's *Incarnate* and *Night of the Claw,"* in *Studies in Weird Fiction* no. 6 (Fall 1989): 3-9.

Proulx, Kevin E. "Ramsey Campbell," in *Fear to the World: Eleven Voices in a Chorus of Horror.* Mercer Island, WA: Starmont House, 1992, p. 11-33.

"Ramsey Campbell," in *Contemporary Literary Criticism, Volume 42.* Detroit: Gale Research Co., 1987, p. 82-93.

Sullivan, Jack. "Ramsey Campbell: No Light Ahead," in *Shadowings: The Reader's Guide to Horror Fiction, 1981-1982,* edited by Douglas E. Winter. Mercer Island, WA: Starmont House, 1983, p. 79-86.

Sullivan, Jack. "Ramsey Campbell: Premier Stylist," in *Fantasy Reader's Guide to Ramsey Campbell.* Wallsend, Tyne & Wear, England: Cosmos Literary Agency, 1980.

Vine, Philip. "Ramsey Campbell: Interview," in *Interzone* no. 28 (March/April 1989): 11-16.

Wiater, Stanley. "A Conversation with Ramsey Campbell," in *Twilight Zone* 7 (April 1987): 88-89.

Wiater, Stanley. "Ramsey Campbell," in *Dark Dreamers: Conversations with the Masters of Horror.* New York: Avon, 1990, p. 35-42.

Winter, Douglas E. "Ramsey Campbell," in *Faces of Fear.* New York: Berkley Books, 1985, p. 65-78.

III.

DENNIS ETCHISON

A DENNIS ETCHISON CHRONOLOGY

1943 Dennis William Etchison born March 30 at Stockton, California.

1949 Etchison family moves to Los Angeles.

1961 First professional sale, "Odd Boy Out," published in *Escapade*.

1963 Attends a writing workshop in science fiction taught by Charles Beaumont at UCLA; Attends UCLA film school about the same time.

1965 "Wet Season" published in *Gamma* no. 5, (September); "The Country of the Strong" published in *New Writings in SF 4*, edited by John Carnell (Dobson, UK).

1968 "Bright Are the Stars That Shine, Dark Is the Sky" published in *New Writings in SF 11*, edited by John Carnell (Dobson, UK).

1974 "The Soft Wall" published in *Whispers* no. 4, (July); "Black Sun" published in *Orbit 13*, edited by Damon Knight (Putnam).

1979 "The Dead Line" published in *Whispers* nos. 13/14, (October); "It Will Be Here Soon" published in *Weirdbook* no. 14.

1980 Movie novelization, *The Fog*, published by Bantam.

1981 "The Dark Country" published in *Fantasy Tales*, Summer; movie novelization, *Halloween II*, published under pseudonym JACK MARTIN.

1982 "The Dark Country" (story) wins British Fantasy Award and World Fantasy Award; *The Dark Country* (collection) published by Scream/Press, the book sells out four printings, quite remarkable for a story collection by an author with no novels to his credit; movie novelizations, *Videodrome* (Zebra) and *Halloween III* (Jove) published under pseudonym JACK MARTIN.

1983 *The Dark Country* nominated for the World Fantasy Award.

1984 *Red Dreams* (collection) published by Scream/Press.

1986   *Darkside* (first novel, besides movie novelizations) published by Charter; *Cutting Edge* (anthology) released by Doubleday; *Masters of Darkness* (anthology) published by Tor.

1988   *The Blood Kiss* (collection) published by Scream/Press; *Lord John 10: A Celebration* (anthology) published by Lord John Press; *Masters of Darkness II* (anthology) published by Tor.

1989   *The Blood Kiss* nominated for World Fantasy Award.

1991   *The Complete Masters of Darkness* (anthology incorporating the first two anthologies and the first appearance of the latter) published by Underwood-Miller; *Masters of Darkness III* published as a separate book by Tor.

1992   *MetaHorror* (anthology) published by Dell Abyss.

1993   *MetaHorror* reprinted by Donald M. Grant; *Shadow Man* (novel) published by Dell Abyss.

A DENNIS ETCHISON INTERVIEW

SCHWEITZER: Could you give us some background about yourself? How long have you been writing and what were you doing before then?

ETCHISON: I've always been writing, since the time I was about ten or eleven. I had a teacher in the sixth grade who required a composition of some sort every week, and there were a couple of other boys in the class along with me who were budding writers, and we would turn in a short story every week. That was the training that started me. When I was twelve I was fortunate enough to win $250 in an "Americanism" essay contest that the Elks Lodge sponsored. That taught me that you could get money for writing, which spoiled me. I made my first story sale, professionally, when I was seventeen, in 1960, and I've been doing it ever since, only fairly recently making a decent living at it.

SCHWEITZER: In the '60s, you seemed to appear rather infrequently. Did you write little or were you unable to sell all you wrote?

ETCHISON: There's probably more than most people are aware of, but if you're going strictly from a science fiction index you get the idea there were only a few. There were more, in men's magazines and little magazines, that most people don't know about. A few of those have been reprinted now, but not many. As a matter of fact, I've never been very prolific, but there aren't quite as many big gaps in the chronology as you would guess.

SCHWEITZER: Do you want these early stories reprinted, or are you being selective?

ETCHISON: There are a couple, I suppose, that should be buried. The problem arises, when you come to reprint stories, that times have changed so and your own awareness of language has changed so that there are some lines that you simply can't let get through in a new reprint. I can remember a line in a story that I wrote when I was nineteen. It said of a girl something like "she felt suddenly gay." Now you can't get away with that now, but in 1962 or whenever that was, that word didn't have as much currency as it has now. So, when that story came to be reprinted, I had to make a few changes. It's a great temptation to go back and rewrite those stories. I would prefer not to. I would like to leave them essentially as they were, as representations of what I did, which was the best that I could do at that particular time, but it's hard to do it. You have to grit your teeth. Bradbury, of course, spent a lot of time rewriting the stories from *Dark Carnival* for *The October Country*, and other stories like "King of the Grey Spaces." And in some cases, I find the original published versions to be more moving and more intense because they had a certain *naiveté* and emotional rush to them that you don't get in the very polished and metered prose of his later years.

SCHWEITZER: During this period were you somewhat discouraged from writing horror fiction for want of a market?

ETCHISON: I don't want to sound pompous, but I honestly have never considered the market when I wrote. I've never written a story on order, and I've never written a story that was slanted to a particular publisher. Many times I've been asked for stories over the years, and if I had a story that I had finished or that I was working on which would be appropriate to the magazine or anthology in question, I would send it along, but I have never been able to sit down and write one to order. Frequently, when I've started stories, I did not know whether they were going to be fantasy, science fiction, horror, or contemporary stories. I wrote what I felt I most wanted to write at that moment, and *then* I began the marketing process. They were two distinct processes. They weren't related at all. Fifty percent of me was trying to be the pure artist at the typewriter, and once it was finished it became the product to be marketed. I handled it in quite a different way. So, to answer your question, I never really thought about the markets, which is one of the reasons, I suppose, why it took me so long to make a living.

SCHWEITZER: Is the reason you can't write to order that the whole spontaneity of the creative process is gone when you try to?

ETCHISON: It just seems that writing is the one area of life that should be pure and free. Every other job is essentially doing what someone else wants you to do in order to get money, and writing to order is really no different from working in a gas station or washing dishes. I would rather that this one area of my life be as pure as possible. There have been a few compromises in order to survive, but I hope there won't be any more.

SCHWEITZER: What if the editor says, "Our readers don't like downbeat endings. Change the ending and I'll buy it"? What do you do?

ETCHISON: Many times I've received recommendations from editors. In one case, I remember an editor wanted me to take out the first twelve pages of the story, which was about twenty-four pages in length, but I didn't do it, and sold it elsewhere, and it was later reprinted four or five times. Many times I get suggestions, sometimes very detailed suggestions. I read them over; I think about them; I take out my carbon of the story and read it, and then I sleep on it. If I agree with the suggestion—and sometimes they are right—I go ahead and do it, but if I really don't think it is an improvement I don't do it. I think Alfred Bester once said "The book is king," which is a way of saying that your only commitment is to the quality of your work. If a suggestion is good for the story, then I'll change it. If it's not, I won't. Sometimes they buy it anyway. Sometimes I have to peddle it somewhere else.

SCHWEITZER: Certainly you are best known now for your horror fiction. What is the attraction of this field for you? Were you trying to write in it from the beginning?

ETCHISON: I don't know. I've always sold my things to whomever would buy them, and it's just been coincidental in the last four or five years that so many pieces have appeared in horror collections and magazines. I hope I'm not slanting them in that direction unconsciously. In the '60s I used to try to do a mainstream story followed by a science fiction story followed by a fantasy, in order to keep things balanced out, so I would not fall into one camp or the other. The disadvantage of that is that you don't build up a following among the audience because your work is spread thinly over a wide area, but the advantage is that you don't find yourself making unconscious adjustments to suit the market. For example, the people who think of themselves only as science fiction writers tend to take their original inspirational impulses, and in some cases, I think, bend them or shift them unconsciously in order to make them into science fiction stories. A lot of science fiction stories have no reason to be set in the future or on another planet, but the author does it because that's what he does. I want to use science fiction or fantasy or horror or whatever the genre is only so far as it's appropriate to the particular inspiration. If a story did not call for a supernatural element I would not put it in. I would write it as mainstream.

SCHWEITZER: Were you originally turned on to horror fiction by the comic books of the 1950s? I suspect they've had an influence on your whole generation, directly and indirectly.

ETCHISON: My mother would never let me buy EC comics, back before Dr. Wertham. I can remember sneaking a peek at a few of them at friends' homes, but I was never permitted to have horror stories in the house. It was only a few years later that I discovered them and devoured them and loved them. So I guess, yeah, I was influenced by Feldstein and Wood and Davis and all those wonderful artists of EC comics in the early '50s. Also by movies. A lot by movies. My earliest recollections of the horror genre would be not from EC comics, but from films. I can remember, for example, a scene from a picture that I later found out was *Hurricane Island* with Jon Hall, made in the '40s, in which a young woman suddenly aged horribly, *à la Lost Horizon*, and I've never forgotten that. I can see it as vividly now as if it had happened a month or two ago. Visual imagery is where it's coming from. That's the point. I'm not coming from a background of Lovecraft. I'm not coming from a background of the older genre books, but more from the visual media, and also from Bradbury. Think of the Bradbury stories from the '40s, the *Dark Carnival* stories, the *Illustrated Man* stories, the *October Country* stories. That was really the strongest influence on me. Bradbury was the strongest influence, and I'm sure still is. It took many years to break away from that.

SCHWEITZER: Where do the visual images you use come from, except from movies?

ETCHISON: The visual aspect, I guess, would make me an imagist in terms of schools of poetry, and I've also felt much closer to poetry than I have to the novel, which may be why I write short stories, not novels, and may be why I find myself working in the screenplay form lately. The screenplay, after all, is just a description of visual images. Someone once said that science fiction is closer to poetry and surrealism than other forms of literature, and I think that's true. Science fiction, at its very best, is visionary and at the cutting edge of the surrealist movement.

SCHWEITZER: Do you see horror fiction as visionary, perhaps, in some inward-looking sense?

ETCHISON: It seems to me that horror fiction—good horror fiction—is an attempt to come to terms, to say what's *really* there. It doesn't skirt the issue. It doesn't place it in the future. It doesn't romanticize it. A story such as my "Dead Line" is an attempt to really come to grips with some serious issues, and not to pull any punches, to describe the consequences as accurately as possible. Good horror fiction, I think, is the opposite of escapist fiction. It is an attempt to bring you closer to reality. As a result I find that I don't like elfinland/fairyland books at all, and I don't like Lovecraft at all, who always pulls back a bit at the end and gets vague and mysterious about the nameless, shapeless form that was too hideous to describe. That seems to me a retreat into a safe cop-out. What I'm trying to do is to see what's really there. What William Burroughs means when, in *Naked Lunch*, he referred to "that moment when everyone sees what is at the end of every fork."

SCHWEITZER: The nameless hideous thing *is* a cop-out, but what Lovecraft was doing, or at least what he thought he was doing, was depicting Mankind against a larger framework. Do you think it is detrimental to the effectiveness of the story to get beyond the individual, to, so to speak, pull the camera back till you see the crowd?

ETCHISON: I just don't see the necessity for it. If your eyes and ears are really open during the day, you're going to confront the consequences of reality, and what you see and hear is going to be so distressing that to invent the Ancient Ones is essentially irrelevant. There is evil in the world, but in beginning to deal with it, we have to begin with the evil that's closest at hand and move on from there. Pulling back and digging deeper, I realize that this position about Lovecraft is a very dangerous one to take in this field at this moment. A writer like Ramsey Campbell, for example, comes very much from a Lovecraftian tradition. He's surpassed it, transcended it, and he is, in fact, my favorite writer in this field. But you'll notice that all of Ramsey's mature work is concerned with that which lurks beneath the surface of everyday life. That seems to me to be so much more disturbing than an abstract concept of an ancient evil from the bowels of the Earth.

SCHWEITZER: What about Poe?

ETCHISON: Poe's short stories were very fine. They were obsessive-compulsive works, and I think his various problems are very easily discernable in the symbols he uses: incest, drinking, drug addiction, and so forth. I don't find that same sort of veiled avoidance as I do in Lovecraft and in the Lovecraft followers. The Lovecraft school has done more to hold back the development of modern Dark Fantasy than any other group or individual writer, just as Pound and Eliot have probably done more to hold back advancements in poetry than any other poets.

SCHWEITZER: You mentioned earlier that you write stories from images. Do you ever get these from dreams? Do you write stories based on dreams?

ETCHISON: I'm glad you asked that. Not only do I write from dreams, I have dreamed entire stories and seen them typed out before my eyes. Two or three times I woke myself up in the middle of the night, grabbed pencil and paper, and copied down as many lines as I could remember, sometimes skipping pages and filling in the shape of paragraphs, and filling in an occasional word whenever I could remember it, sometimes entire lines and paragraphs. But I dream the entire story typed out in manuscript form. This happened to me three or four times over the years. I would see the pages turning. I've sold those stories. Many times I dream experientially, and these events are described in short stories, but what really fascinates me is the dreamed manuscript, and I would like to know if other writers have encountered this phenomenon. If so, it might be productive to put together an anthology of such stories. Have you ever heard of anything like this?

SCHWEITZER: I've heard that David H. Keller used to dream them one page at a time. [NOTE: See introduction to his *Tales from Underwood.*—D.S.]

ETCHISON: It's much more convenient that way because you have more time to get them down.

SCHWEITZER: When you are writing such a story, is it as if you are transcribing the work of someone else, and it's in ink which fades as you go along?

ETCHISON: Some writers seem to work almost entirely visually. Phil Dick has said that when he types he sees a small stage a few feet in front of his typewriter, like a window, and he sees small puppet-sized characters walking in and out of the room, and what he's doing is essentially describing the action like a playwright, what he sees transpiring on the miniature stage. It's not that neat and compact for me. I see it all around me, like Cinerama. A lot of times you get involved with the language itself, and it will lead you onto a trip in and of itself, one word suggesting another, rather in the way a poet would work. Other times you're writing fast and attempting to get down the action that you see. Colors are also very important, sounds, all the senses. I think it was Poul Anderson who said a few years ago that he used to include all the five senses in at least key passages of his books, so the reader could taste and smell and see, etc. what was happening and it would seem more real. The most obvious expression of this would be Ray Bradbury, who is the most sensory writer I can think of. This can be carried to excess. It is sometimes interesting to do something perverse and work in the opposite direction. I've done stories in which there are very deliberately no colors at all until the very end, and you suddenly have a mention of color for the first time. The idea is that it will be like a burst of color footage at the end of a black-and-white movie. The reader ideally would not know *why* the ending was effective, but it would seem extraordinarily vivid to him. This is all shop-talk and it doesn't really matter. It's like the preparations that a magician makes behind the scenes. It doesn't really matter what he does to produce the effect. The only thing that counts is the illusion that the audience sees.

SCHWEITZER: How do you think this mechanism works? Are they whole stories coming out of the unconscious, or are you getting parts which you consciously string together into a story?

ETCHISON: When the going gets tough, I go through my notebooks and pull out lines and images collected over the years that seem to relate to each other in some way and build a story around them. Usually that doesn't happen. The explanation is probably that the good stories are coming almost directly out of the unconscious. But it may not be the unconscious. It may be some sort of super- or hyper-consciousness because you're really cooking at the machine. It's as if some force is moving your hands and you're not really aware of having decided what's going to happen next. It's as if you're merely the conduit for a story that is already carefully formed and exists on another plane. It's passing through you and you're just the instrument for recording it. It's a very strange feeling indeed, but it happens. Sometimes the characters come alive and write their own stories. As you know, Sturgeon killed off Zena in *The Dreaming Jewels* only to find that he loved her so much he couldn't leave her dead. So he brought her back to life later on in the book. Many times characters will write their own stories because they become so real to you that they take on autonomy. Many times stories of mine turn out quite differently than I'd imagined they would, because the characters have certain needs that I couldn't have anticipated. Bradbury once described plot as the footprints that are left in the snow after the characters have run past on their way to whatever it is they're after. The writer is simply the person who comes along and records the footsteps.

SCHWEITZER: Can you prime this unconscious pump to work whenever you want it to?

ETCHISON: Those are the tricks of the trade. That's what you spend years trying to get yourself to do. There are all sorts of little tricks that wouldn't make sense to anyone else. I'm sure every writer has his own ritual he goes through. For myself, I try to trick myself into believing that I'm doing something else. And before I know it, there are three or four pages by the typewriter. I say that I'm going to do a certain number of hours at the typewriter tomorrow because I've been putting it off for weeks, it won't get done, because my unconscious will throw up all sorts of excuses, other jobs that have to be done that I hadn't thought of. The only way to do it is to pretend that you're going to do something else and make sure you have the right number of hours available. Then you go through these warm-up exercises and tricks of the trade. Learning to prime the pump and to get this flow going is what being a professional writer is all about, and a productive professional is someone who is able to do this during the hours available to him. If you sit around and wait for inspiration to strike, you'll produce nothing. That's the difference between being an amateur and a professional.

SCHWEITZER: You mean it has nothing to do with quality, just the ability to get the job done?

ETCHISON: No, it is a question of quality. What separates the talented amateur from the professional is the *ability* to produce good work on a regular basis when the time is available, not just when inspiration strikes. If you work only from inspiration, you'll always be an amateur, no matter how good your work is.

SCHWEITZER: Do you write a regular number of hours a day?

ETCHISON: As Mickey Spillane said, "When I write." He brags of turning out ten or twenty single-spaced pages on the typewriter a day. But that's *when* he writes. When I'm working on a story, I try to do four or five pages a day until it's finished. Sometimes the whole story gets finished in a day or two. Of course it's different if I'm working under a deadline, like I did with *The Fog*. I had exactly six weeks to the day to do that book, and I wanted to do two drafts of it; the manuscript was about 285 pages. Because I type with one finger, that required a lot of work. So I found myself sitting at the typewriter twelve to fourteen hours a day, seven days a week, for six weeks. I remember getting on the train to come to the World Fantasy Convention in Providence. I met someone and told her that I was a writer. She said, "Oh, that must be such interesting work." And I said, "Quite honestly, it's awful. I haven't seen the sun for six weeks." And it was true.

SCHWEITZER: Could you imagine yourself as something other than a writer?

ETCHISON: I don't particularly like writing. I never have. It's always been my third or fourth choice in life. When I was ten I decided that I wanted to direct movies more than anything else in the world, and I've never changed that opinion. A great many people of my generation feel the same way. I went to UCLA Film School in the 1960s, and I have pursued the field obsessively over the years, but very little has come of it. I'm also much more interested in photography than I am in writing, but writing is the only one of these areas to present me with any outlet so far. What I'd like to do ideally, and the only reason I'm working in screenplays at the moment—it's a kind of ersatz writing, very unsatisfying—is to write a couple of successful low budget horror screenplays, and then tell them they can have the next one for free if I can direct it. That's essentially what I want to do. I love literature; I love books; but writing really doesn't satisfy me. It just happens to be the only thing I have an outlet for.

SCHWEITZER: Are you satisfied with *having written*, when you look at your own work afterwards?

ETCHISON: I'm sure every writer who looks back at his old work is embarrassed. I look at the early stories as if they were written by someone else. It's very hard to imagine that I wrote them. They seem to me to be very interesting, eccentric, intuitive works by someone with talent but very little technique. Some of the more recent stories I've read when they come out—this may be a year or two later—and I still have that feeling that someone else wrote them, but I think to myself, "Yeah, that's a pretty fair country story." And then it's pleasing to see my name on them. Once the story is finished, once the final draft is typed, Xeroxed, and filed, a great dissociation or detachment sets in, and I find that I no longer view them subjectively. As I say, it's as if someone else wrote them.

SCHWEITZER: Will you regard your present work this way in a couple years?

ETCHISON: I hope that as I go on each story will be less and less disappointing, that I'll be getting closer and closer to the mark. But I suppose, now that you mention it, that what I think is a good story now will probably be revealed to be a very inadequate story five years from now. I hope that's not the case, but I suppose it's inevitable.

A SELECT SECONDARY BIBLIOGRAPHY ON DENNIS ETCHISON

Kiplinger, Christine. "Interview: Dennis Etchison," in *Science Fiction Chronicle* 5 (May, 1984): 1, 19-20.

Morrison, Michael A. "Horror Author Profile: Dennis Etchison," in *Science Fiction & Fantasy Book Review Annual 1989*, edited by Robert A. Collins and Robert Latham. Westport, CT: Meckler, 1990, p. 106-109.

"SF, Fantasy, Horror Writing Class in LA," in *Science Fiction Chronicle* 5 (January, 1984): 4, 6.

Stamm, M. E. "The Dark Side of the American Dream: Dennis Etchison," in *Discovering Modern Horror Fiction I*, edited by Darrell Schweitzer. Mercer Island, WA: Starmont House, 1985, p. 48-55.

Wagner, Karl Edward. "Dennis Etchison: The Unknown Writer," in *Shadowings: The Reader's Guide to Horror Fiction, 1981-1982*, edited by Douglas E. Winter. Mercer Island, WA: Starmont House, 1983, p. 87-91.

Wagner, Karl Edward. "On Fantasy," in *Fantasy Newsletter* 6 (February, 1983): 8-10.

Wiater, Stanley. "Dennis Etchison," in *Dark Dreamers: Conversations with the Masters of Horror*. New York: Avon, 1990, p. 51-58.

Wiater, Stanley. "On the Cutting Edge: A Conversation with Dennis Etchison," in *Twilight Zone* 7 (February, 1988): 20-23.

Winter, Douglas E. "Dennis Etchison," in *Faces of Fear*. New York: Berkley Books, 1985, p. 50-64.

IV.

CHARLES L. GRANT

A CHARLES L. GRANT CHRONOLOGY

1942   Charles L. Grant born September 12 at Newark, New Jersey.

1964   Receives B.A. from Trinity College, Hartford, Connecticut.

1964-68 Teaches English at Toms River High School, New Jersey.

1968   First published story, "The House of Evil," in *The Magazine of Fantasy and Science Fiction* (December).

1968-70 Serves in U.S. Army military police, in Vietnam; awarded Bronze Star.

1970-72 Teaches English at Chester High School, New Jersey.

1972-73 Teaches English at Mt. Olive High School, New Jersey.

1973   "The Summer of the Irish Sea" published in *Orbit 11*, edited by Damon Knight; "The Magic Child" published in *Frontiers 2*, edited by Roger Elwood; "Weep No More, Old Lady," published in *Future Quest*, edited by Roger Elwood; "Abdication" published in *Amazing Science Fiction Stories*, (October).

1973-77 Secretary of Science Fiction Writers of America.

1973   Marries Debbie Voss (divorced; Grant later remarries novelist Kathryn Ptacek).

1976   Wins Nebula Award for "A Crowd of Shadows"; *The Curse* published by Major Books; *The Shadow of Alpha* published by Berkley Books.

1977   *Ascension* published by Berkley Books; *The Hour of the Oxrun Dead* published by Doubleday; *Writing and Selling Science Fiction* (nonfiction anthology, edited by Grant) published by Writer's Digest Books.

1978   *The Ravens of the Moon* and *The Sound of Midnight* published by Doubleday; first volume of *Shadows* anthology series published by Doubleday; *Nightmares* (anthology) published by Doubleday; *The Hour of the Oxrun Dead* is a finalist for the World Fantasy Award as Best Novel; wins Nebula Award for Best Novelette with "A Glow of Candles, A Unicorn's Eye."

1979   *Legion* published by Berkley Books; *The Last Call of Mourning* published by Doubleday; *The Sound of Midnight* finalist for the World Fantasy Award in Best Novel category; "Come To Me Now, My Sweet Abbey Rose" finalist for World Fantasy Award as Best Short Story; *Shadows* wins World Fantasy Award for Best Anthology/Collection; *Riverrun*, first of several romance novels, published under pseudonym FELICIA ANDREWS.

1980   *The Last Call of Mourning* finalist for the World Fantasy Award for Best Novel; *Nightmares* and *Shadows 2* are finalists for the World Fantasy Award for Best Anthology.

1981   *Tales from the Nightside: Dark Fantasy* published by Arkham House; *A Glow of Candles and Other Stories* published by Berkley Books; *The Grave* published by Popular Library; *Horrors* (anthology) published by Doubleday; *Shadows 3* is a finalist for the World Fantasy Award.

1982   *The Nestling* published by Pocket Books; *The Soft Whisper of the Dead* published by Donald M. Grant; *Nightmare Seasons* published by Doubleday; *Terrors* (anthology) published by Pocket Books; "Coin of the Realm" is a finalist for the World Fantasy Award for Best Short Story; *Shadows 4* and *Tales from the Nightside* are finalists for the World Fantasy Award for Best Anthology/Collection.

1983   *The Dodd, Mead Gallery of Horror* anthology is published by Dodd, Mead; *Fears* (anthology) published by Berkley; "Confess the Seasons" wins the World Fantasy Award for Best Novella; *The Nestling* is a finalist for the World Fantasy Award for Best Novel; *Nightmare Seasons* wins the World Fantasy Award for Best Anthology/Collection; *Shadows 5* is a finalist for the World Fantasy Award.

1984   *Night Songs* published by Pocket Books; *King of Satan's Eyes* (as by GEOFFREY MARSH) published by Doubleday; *Shadows 6* and *The Dodd, Mead Gallery of Horror* are finalists for the World Fantasy Award.

1985   *The Tea Party* published by Pocket Books; *Midnight* (anthology) published by Tor; *Night Visions 2* (anthology; editors in this series change with each volume) published by Dark Harvest; *Greystone Bay* (shared-setting anthology, edited by Grant) published by Tor; *The Orchard* published by Tor; *The Dark Cry of the Moon* published by Donald M. Grant; *Blood River Down* (QUEST OF THE WHITE DUCK TRILOGY #1, as by LIONEL FENN) published by Ace/Berkley.

1986   *The Tail of the Arabian Knight* (as by GEOFFREY MARSH) published by Doubleday; *Web of Defeat* and *Agnes Day* (WHITE DUCK #2 and #3, as by LIONEL FENN) published by Ace/Berkley; *Night Visions 2* is a finalist for the World Fantasy Award; *The Pet* published by Tor; *The Long Night in the Grave* published by Donald M. Grant; *Black Wine*, (a Grant/Ramsey Campbell anthology, edited by Douglas Winter), published by Dark Harvest.

1987 *For Fear in the Night* published by Tor; *The Patch of the Odin Soldier* (as by GEOFFREY MARSH) published by Doubleday; *The Pet* is a finalist for the World Fantasy Award for Best Novel.

1988 *Fangs of the Hooded Demon* (as by GEOFFREY MARSH) published by Tor.

1989 *In a Dark Dream* and *Dialing the Wind* published by Tor.

1990 *Stunts* published by Tor; *In a Dark Dream* is a finalist for the World Fantasy Award for Best Novel; *The Sealharp Hotel* (GREYSTONE BAY ANTHOLOGY #3) published by Tor; *Kent Montana and the Really Ugly Thing* (as by LIONEL FENN) published by Ace.

1991 *Final Shadows* (11th in series) published by Doubleday; *Something Stirs* published by Tor; *Fire Mask* published by Bantam; *Kent Montana and the Once and Future Thing* and *Kent Montana and the Reasonably Invisible Man* (as by LIONEL FENN) published by Ace.

1992 *668: The Neighbor of the Beast* and *The Mark of the Moderately Vicious Vampire* (as by LIONEL FENN) published by Ace

1993 *Once Upon a Time in the East* (as by LIONEL FENN) published by Ace; *Raven* and *In the Fog* (anthology) published by Tor.

1994 *By the Time I Get to Nashville* (as by LIONEL FENN) published by Ace.

A CHARLES L. GRANT INTERVIEW

SCHWEITZER: What do you think about the state of contemporary supernatural horror fiction?

GRANT: In terms of markets, I guess, it's better than it's been in the last ten years, obviously. In terms of payment, it's not much better, if you talk about short fiction. In terms of novels, it's easier to sell a supernatural horror novel than it has ever been. For novels, the money's better; publicity is better; subsidiary rights are better. Pretty damn good. In terms of quality, the same as always. It's just like science fiction. Out of every ten horror novels published in a year, either in hardback or paperback, maybe three of them are worth reading.

SCHWEITZER: How is the field doing in terms of subject matter? Isn't there a danger of stagnation? Now, the pre-Lovecraftian stories give us the classic ghosts and vampires, and the post-Lovecraftian ones give us the Things-From-Outside and the like. Both can become clichés.

GRANT: One of the things that contemporary writers are doing is mining different mythologies for their monsters or witches or whatever. American Indians are "in" now. *Prophecy*, for example, which was a God-awful movie. The book wasn't bad. But American Indians are "in." I had one a long time ago—and I'm trying to buy up all the copies and hide it—that was based on an American Indian myth about Tecumseh.. I did the book wrong, but it was my first one. I'm writing a new one now, based on Shoshone Indian myth, which will be much better. So there are other mythologies. Norse, African, etc. Also, modern writers are creating new ones. That's important to avoid stagnation.

SCHWEITZER: But you can still run into problems. Seabury Quinn exploited every mythology conceivable for Jules de Grandin, and the results always came out the same.

GRANT: The thing is to twist it. It's like Chelsea Quinn Yarbro's vampire. There are just so many things you can write about a vampire, but Yarbro has set her vampire up on a timeline that starts with Genghis Khan's China and goes up through the two World Wars. And her vampire is a hero. Fred Saberhagen's trio of Dracula novels have Dracula as the hero, not a villain. You take what is familiar and twist it. I've written one werewolf story and two vampire stories. In the werewolf story, the werewolf feeds on failure. In one of the vampire stories, the vampire feeds on affection, emotion. The vampire has sex with its victim and continues to do so until all emotion is totally drained, whereupon the victim becomes a vampire and carries on. There's no drinking of blood or any of that.

SCHWEITZER: I can see why that hasn't been done before. It wouldn't have been publishable twenty years ago.

GRANT: No, and it wasn't when I first wrote it [*laughs*].

SCHWEITZER: Once someone asked you what was the major source of supernatural horror in modern literature, and you said "children."

GRANT: Oh, yes. Stephen King and I have had a running argument about this since we met. King believes that children are basically Good with a capital "G." And he was a teacher, also, which is why I can't understand this. I don't think that children are basically bad, or evil. Children are just so totally amoral that they are about the worst things you could possibly conceive in the entire universe. Children are vicious and nasty and cruel and have no compunctions about doing whatever I have them doing to adults in my stories. And they always win. The adults are bound by moral decisions and the fact that they don't know what reality is. Children do.

SCHWEITZER: Do you have any children?

GRANT: I have two. A boy and a girl, and they're no different than any other kids. They're so young—one is three and a half; the other is a year and a half—they are just amoral. Vicious, nasty little beasts.

SCHWEITZER: So they would be more effective than Lovecraft's squammous Things?

GRANT: Oh, yes, sure. Because kids are all over the place. It is easier to imagine a child than to imagine some slime thing that rises out of the sea. I didn't start writing until I was twenty-six, but when I was in high school, for some reason or other, I wrote in a little loose-leaf notebook a story about these things that came out of a swamp, and they were hairy—they looked kind of like mastodons without trunks—and they thudded out of this swamp, destroyed a little town, and thudded back into the swamp again. I think it was all of thirty of those tiny pages, and I would pass those pages around to my history class. Every day I would come in with a new page. I don't know *why* I did it.

SCHWEITZER: I remember doing something like that in high school. Everybody thought it was thrilling.

GRANT: I went to a more sophisticated high school.

SCHWEITZER: That must be it. My story was about man-eating leprechauns who got away with it because of the good press leprechauns always get.

GRANT: That's a perfect example of what I'm talking about. I can't tell you much about it, but I've got an idea for a novel about Merlin which is going to be the exact opposite of what everybody thinks Merlin is, and it'll be a horror novel. You can work with that. You take a leprechaun. Everybody thinks a leprechaun is really neat and it sells Trix or whatever the hell those things are.

SCHWEITZER: Lucky Charms [a breakfast cereal].

GRANT: Yeah, and if you can turn such a preconceived notion into something absolutely against the grain, but hide it until the end of the story—that's the key, that you hide the true nature of whatever it is you're working with until the very end of the story, so that the ending is doubly powerful if it's done right. I don't like to guess what's going to happen at the beginning of the story unless I can be convinced that I guessed wrong, which is nice.

SCHWEITZER: You also have to avoid lying to the reader. As an editor you must rather frequently get the story in which you get to the end and discover the guy is a lobster or something.

GRANT: No, no, that's not what I'm talking about at all. A good supernatural horror story is like a mystery. All the clues are there. The reader *may not necessarily pick them up* until the end, and then he can think back and say, "Oh, yes, of course!" But no, cheating is out. And I hate stories that cheat. Novels that cheat are even worse.

SCHWEITZER: There's one thing that Bram Stoker did very well which the post-Lovecraftian school doesn't. Well we won't mention names, but...

GRANT: Go ahead.

SCHWEITZER: Okay, let's suppose that August Derleth had written *Dracula* in a pseudo-Lovecraftian style. It would be about four chapters long written in the First Person Delirious, and the ultimate shocking revelation, in italics, would have been, *He was a vampire!!!!* It would have been an aborted beginning. But it seems to me that many of the best stories take the surprise and use it as the beginning and go on from there. As Stoker did.

GRANT: Yes, or as King did in *'Salem's Lot*. Seventy-five pages into the book I knew it was about vampires. But go from that to the quality of the writing. In spite of the fact that most people know that the book is about vampires, fifty or seventy-five pages into this 450-page book, the man is so good at writing about people—and that's the big difference between horror and science fiction—that you keep going anyway, because you know so much about these people that you can't wait to see who's going to get it and who's not. The *big* thing about *'Salem's Lot* is the fact that the *heroine* gets it, and when she gets nailed by the vampire, the reaction of the reader is, "Jesus Christ, *nobody* is safe!" Usually, as in *Dracula*, the heroine's sister will get it, but the hero and the heroine are inviolate. *Wrong.* In *'Salem's Lot* the *heroine* gets it. So you really don't know then, until the very end, who's going to survive. The priest doesn't survive. The best friend doesn't survive. The English teacher doesn't survive. It's only the man and the little boy who do. But even having read the prologue, and knowing that the man and the boy have survived, there is always that element of doubt to the very end, and even at the end there is no guarantee that all the vampires have been killed. And I know something you don't know.

SCHWEITZER: What?

GRANT: I'll never tell.

SCHWEITZER: The sequel in which the little boy....Ah, but to change the subject, why do you have such an intense loathing for Lovecraft?

GRANT: Most people that I know who like Lovecraft started reading him when they were young, early teens or pre-teens. I never read any Lovecraft until I got out of college. I found him immensely unreadable. I can read eighteenth-century British novels with no problem. Lovecraft, I can't touch. He is overwritten and he doesn't frighten me. I am not frightened by huge, slimy things with unpronounceable names. That's not frightening to me.

SCHWEITZER: What scares you?

GRANT: Children...anything in the right circumstances. Any kind of monster will do. I am a horror movie buff. Where I live the drive-ins in the summer will usually get the grade-Z horror movies that show up two months later on television. But I'll go see them and I'll do my damnedest to let them frighten me, even though some of the stuff is really stupid. Just for the hell of it. So anything can scare me if it's done right. What doesn't frighten me are plastic monsters, tentacles, and all that kind of shit. People who are not what they seem frighten me. Then there was *Alien*. *Alien* unnerved me considerably. It was one of the top three horror movies that I have seen in my life. I don't consider it science fiction. It's a horror movie with a science fictional background. The last hour and fifteen minutes of *Alien* are absolute, unrelieved tension, unlike *Jaws*, which I also liked. But I waited a year for it. I would not go see *Jaws* until everyone else had seen it. I wasn't going to be one of the crowd that ran right out and stood in line. In *Jaws*, after every appearance by the shark, there was an instant switch in mood, a comic line by somebody. Like the only time in the film where the shark showed up without the music, and went swooping over the back of the boat, and Scheider goes backing into the cabin where Robert Shaw is and says, "I think you need a bigger boat." But in *Alien* there is no relief of any tension. The moment they start chasing that thing through the ship, there are no funny lines, no relaxation at all. I had a headache when I was done. I loved it.

SCHWEITZER: Would you go back to see it again?

GRANT: Not for several months, simply because I remember too much. It's too vivid. There are things I'd want blurred before I went back. Otherwise I'd be watching it super-critically. I'd be paying attention to the sets and things like that.

SCHWEITZER: And you might find things wrong with it?

GRANT: I don't nitpick. I don't care. It's an emotional picture. It's like finding nits with *Love Story*. That was the most god-awful thing that ever came down the pike, but it was a damn good film in that it did what it was supposed to do. It got too funny for me after a while, but it did what it was supposed to do for most of the people who saw it. *Alien* is the same way. I'm sure there must be holes in the plot somewhere.

SCHWEITZER: It seemed to me to fall into the old horror movie situation of "Let's separate so it can get us one at a time."

GRANT: It probably did. But so what? A horror movie is not necessarily supposed to be sensible.

SCHWEITZER: What about mixing humor and horror?

GRANT: There's no such thing as a funny horror story. There has to be, depending on the length of the story, some lessening of the tension with *wit*—not humor. Nothing slapstick, in other words. But especially in a long book there should be something to relieve the tension, because a reader can put down a book a lot easier than he can get out of a movie he's paid five bucks to see. So in longer versions there is definitely a need for wit.

SCHWEITZER: Robert Bloch has claimed that humor and horror are two sides of the same coin, since they both deal with the grotesque, and thus they can somewhat overlap.

GRANT: That's true, but still there is no such thing as a funny horror story. A horror story with a punchline is not a horror story. One with a horrifying punchline, but maybe leads up to it with wit, that's okay. But to use ghosts or vampires to get to a joke, that's not horrifying. It's just another way of telling a joke.

SCHWEITZER: Well, consider something like Ramsey Campbell's "Heading Home." I found that to be a funny story, mostly as a literary exercise because it was dancing on the graves of all the horror story rules.

GRANT: I'll tell you how dense I am. The title gave me no clue to what was going on, and when I got to the end, I got it, and I knew what the title meant. I don't pay much attention to titles, unless they are very long, and then I have to.

SCHWEITZER: Well you use very long titles. An editor who shall remain nameless, who didn't like a story of mine, said, "Why don't you use one of those long, arty titles like C. L. Grant uses?"

GRANT: That shows where his head is at. I haven't used "C. L. Grant" in many years.

SCHWEITZER: You don't like Lovecraft. I assume you don't care for the Lovecraft followers either.

GRANT: Yes, that's right. I don't like Brian Lumley. I didn't like Ramsey Campbell in his early stuff because it was too Lovecraftian. There are a lot of contemporary writers I can't stand. Graham Masterson is *terrible*. There is a guy named Bernard Taylor, who has written two books that are really excellent. I assume he's British because his books were first published in Britain. One is called *The Godsend* and the other is *Sweetheart, Sweetheart*, and it's the best ghost story I have ever read in my life. That even includes Peter Straub's book, *Ghost Story*, which is also excellent. But unfortunately, it relies too heavily on what he is trying to do, which is make a literary event out of a horror novel. There are too many obvious bows to Hawthorne, to Stephen King, and Poe, and James. The references are too bald for me. They also blew it with the last line, which was not good. King's wife and I had a long talk about that on the phone, and we both agreed that he really blew it at the end. I won't tell you the end if you haven't read it. It's a good book, a literary book, and with incredibly real characters, but at the end he blew it.

SCHWEITZER: I remember an introduction to an H. R. Wakefield collection in which he said, "I've written my last ghost story. It's a dead art form."

GRANT: I don't think it's a dead art form. It's all in the way you handle it. It's like clichés in science fiction. There are all sorts of clichés in supernatural horror fiction. It all depends on how you take the cliché, set it up so people think, "Aha, here we go with another one of these," but if you are sufficiently good in the quality of your writing, people will let you take them along, always hoping in the back of your mind that you're going to do something different. If you do—it doesn't have to be radically different, just enough—then what you've got is an amazingly successful story, and people say, "Oh he did something *great* and *wonderful!*" But he really didn't. He just took something and twisted it. That's all it takes.

SCHWEITZER: Wakefield was writing about 1962, which was a pretty low period for the field. There was a Russell Kirk book published that year which seemed to drop right out of sight. Sometimes I'm afraid the revival of the field was caused by *The Exorcist* and *Rosemary's Baby*.

GRANT: No, no. *Films* may owe something to them, although I feel that *Rosemary's Baby* is a far, far better film than *The Exorcist*, simply because *The Exorcist* is not a horror movie. It's a *terror*. *Jaws* was a terror film. It's the difference between shock and fear, which, if you buy *Shadows*, you will learn about in depth, because my introduction is a long essay on the subject. King says that a little revulsion is good for the soul, which is true. But *The Exorcist* did not frighten me. *Jaws* did not frighten me. Even *Alien* did not frighten me. But it shocked the hell out of me. It's like the old horror movie cliché in which the girl walks up to the closet, puts her hand on the doorknob, and you *know* there's something behind there, and you say to yourself, "She's really stupid if she opens that door." And she opens it up, and the music gets really loud, and everybody goes "*Ahhhh!*" That's not fear. That's shock. Fear is *Rosemary's Baby*. Fear is knowing those people are witches. Fear is knowing what's happened to Rosemary's baby and watching her progress with this thing in her womb. That's frightening because there are no sudden theatrics with loud music and so on. *The Haunting* is the best movie of that type ever made. *That* was a frightening movie. Absolutely frightening.

SCHWEITZER: Or *The Innocents*.

GRANT: Yes. *The Innocents* with Deborah Kerr. Absolutely frightening. As opposed to shock. *Prophecy* is a shock film. It's also a schlock film.

SCHWEITZER: There are a lot like that. I'm told *The Omen* is screamingly funny in places.

GRANT: I like *The Omen* a lot. It had some beautiful scenes in it. The graveyard scene where Peck and whoever it was with him were chased by those dogs, or when the dog is walking through the house, and all you hear is its claws on the bare floor. Or when the priest is being chased by the wind through the park and the lightening rod comes off the church and skewers him. You know this is going to happen, but that's not shock. It's one long build-up scene, a tension scene, which in the priest's case ends with him being skewered, but still it's a frightening thing because the lightening is herding him toward the church and this inevitable end. And yet in the same film they do something dumb, like the scene where the photographer gets beheaded. When his head flies off in the air, I immediately thought, "Gee! That's a neat-looking phony head." Because you *know* it's fake. I am never that caught up in a movie that I think the blood is real. That's shock and it's phony. It doesn't frighten me. What frightens me is saying that I know what's in Rosemary's womb and I don't want to see it. And if you're smart you never do. Except that—do you know that in the last scene of *Rosemary's Baby*, where the camera moves up to Rosemary and she's singing a lullaby, and it's about to swing over the city, if you look really closely in a theatre—you can't see it in television—you can see the baby mirrored in her eyes? You get just a glimpse of this little devil in the cradle. Neat touch.

SCHWEITZER: Well in Lovecraft's best stories it works this way, with the realization that the universe has become fuzzy around the edges and no longer works by the accepted rules, and may be dissolving on you.

GRANT: Maybe so. I just have this block against Lovecraft's style—except for "The Colour Out of Space." Maybe I can't get through the style to the story; as I said before, monsters with unpronounceable names don't frighten me. It doesn't do a thing for me. Stephen King works for me. Dennis Etchison works for me. He is a superb writer. Peter Straub—not *Ghost Story*, but he wrote one called *If You Could See Me Now*, which is a good possession story. And Bernard Taylor. Of course I have favorites. It's not just a matter of quality.

SCHWEITZER: What is your favorite story among your own work—and why?

GRANT: It's always, without exception, the one I'm working on now (assuming we're talking about horror novels and such). I know that's a pat, writer-type answer, but it's true. You see, I have to scare myself first, before I'll send anything out; so, if I'm not doing better now than I did last time out, I'm not doing well at all. And if I *am* doing better, then I'm growing. And if I'm growing, then *that's* my favorite. Of previously published material, though, I would have to say, *The Last Call of Mourning*. I love my ending. It's really rather disgusting if you take the time to think of the implications to Cyd (the heroine). Stories? Two: "Love-Starved" and "Hear Me Now, My Sweet Abbey Rose."

SCHWEITZER: What is the most important thing you've learned as a writer, either about technique, or simply about being a professional?

GRANT: That if I don't grow, I don't work. If I can't see that I'm better this year than last, I might as well hand it up and go back to teaching. I've also learned about rhythm in writing. When I'm finished with a story (story or novel; again, in horror), I read it aloud. And if a sentence doesn't work in rhythm with the paragraph, the paragraph in rhythm with the page, etc., I redo it. I think that's vital, because if you can catch the reader in a rhythm (however unconscious it is on the reader's part), when you depart from it, you jolt him. And the only time I do that is for effect. The rhythm also works toward another, vastly important part of what I do—the end line. I'll tell you, the agonies I go through just to get the last line exactly the way it should be in the story...I wouldn't wish that on anybody. In fact, very often I spend as much time thinking of a last line as I do on the rest of the story. But, boy, when it works...I love it.

SCHWEITZER: What are your actual writing methods like?

GRANT: I start serious writing (that is, not letters or articles or notes for something) around one in the afternoon. This is when I do the stories/novels that aren't closest to my evil little heart. This, for example, is when I do my science fiction, and the other books that I've done in other *genres* under other names. After a two-hour break for a meal, I start writing again around 7:30 p.m. or so. Here's where I do my hard stuff, the writing I sometimes literally sweat over. This, until about midnight or one a.m. In the actual composition, I write out a complete draft of the story or novel, paying no attention to grammar, spelling (I use a kind of typewriter shorthand here), things like that. I write it as *fast* as I can, just to get the story out. Then I go back and make notes to myself (add a scene here, cut this, etc.) and start the final draft: here's where I work on the rhythm, the dialogue, the description, and the last line(s). What it boils down to, then, is very often I'm working on two books (or stories) at the same time. Fast in the afternoon and slow at night. I used to do it all in longhand, but that's too slow. There's too much I want to write, and write about, so I have to cram as much in as I can. This, by the way, is a typical five-day week.

SCHWEITZER: You have a great interest in films. Have you ever had any connections with Hollywood?

GRANT: No. "A Crowd of Shadows" was going to be an NBC-TV movie, but the deal fell through when the man in charge was bumped to a new executive position. Actually, it turned out fairly well: the treatment I did for the short story I turned into a novel, and sold it to Berkley.

SCHWEITZER: Thank you, Charlie Grant.

A SELECT SECONDARY BIBLIOGRAPHY ON CHARLES L. GRANT

D'Ammassa, Don. "The Subtle Terrors of Charles L. Grant," in *Discovering Modern Horror Fiction II*, edited by Darrell Schweitzer. Mercer Island, WA: Starmont House, 1988, p. 81-87.

Neilson, Keith. "The Oxrun Station Series," in *Survey of Modern Fantasy Literature*, edited by Frank N. Magill. Englewood Cliffs, NJ: Salem Press, 1983, Vol. 3, p. 1191-1195.

Pettus, David. "Charles Grant: Interview," in *American Fantasy* 1 (May, 1982): 17-21.

Wiater, Stanley. "Charles L. Grant," in *Dark Dreamers: Conversations with Masters of Horror*. New York: Avon, 1990, p. 67-74.

Winter, Douglas E. "Charles L. Grant," in *Faces of Fear*. New York: Berkley Books, 1985, p. 108-121.

Winter, Douglas E. "Charles L. Grant: A Profile," in *Science Fiction Review* 14 (November, 1985): 6-9.

Winter, Douglas E. "A Conversation with Charles L. Grant," in *Twilight Zone* 7 (April, 1987): 33, 90-91.

Winter, Douglas E. "Interview: Charles L. Grant," in *Fantasy Newsletter* 5 (January, 1982): 12-15, 34; and 5 (February, 1982): 29-32, 38.

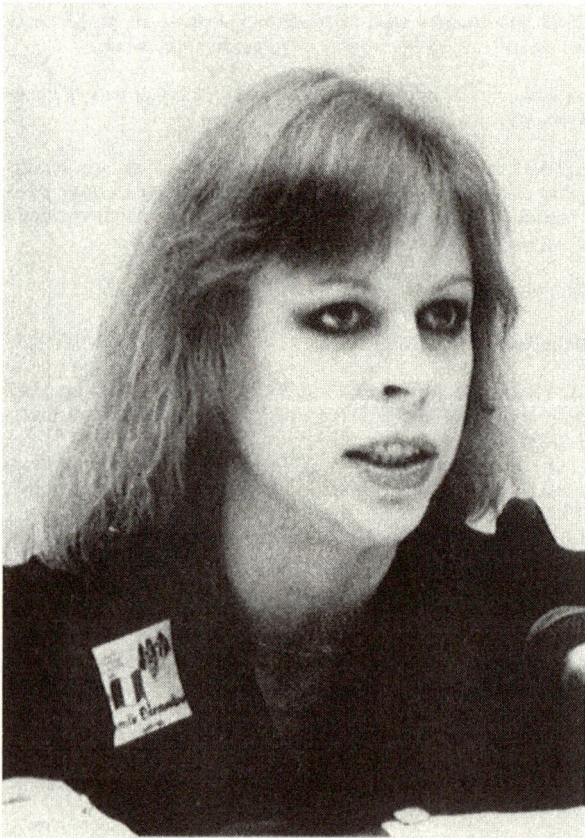

V.

TANITH LEE

A TANITH LEE CHRONOLOGY

1947 Tanith Lee born in London, September 19th.

1950s Educated at Prendergast Grammar School. Later worked as a library assistant, clerk, and waitress in the 1960s.

1971 *The Dragon Hoard* published by Macmillan (London) and Farrar, Straus (New York).

1972 Attends an art college; *Princess Hynchatti and Some Other Surprises* and *Animal Castle* published by Macmillan and Farrar, Straus.

1975 Becomes full-time professional writer; *The Birthgrave* published by DAW; *Companions on the Road* published by Macmillan.

1976 *Don't Bite the Sun* and *The Storm Lord* published by DAW; *The Winter Players* published by Macmillan.

1977 *Drinking Sapphire Wine* and *Volkhavaar* published by DAW; *Companions on the Road and The Winter Players* (combined volume) published by St. Martin's Press; *East of Midnight* published by Macmillan.

1978 *Vazkor, Son of Vazkor, Night's Master*, and *Quest for the White Witch* published by DAW; *Castle of the Dark* published by Macmillan.

1979 *Shon the Taken* published by Macmillan; *Drinking Sapphire Wine* published by Hamlyn; *Electric Forest* and *Death's Master* published by DAW.

1980 *Sabella, or, The Blood Stone, Kill the Dead*, and *Day By Night* published by DAW; teleplay, "Sarcophagus," airs on *Blake's 7*; *Death's Master* wins the August Derleth Award from the British Fantasy Society.

1981 Guest of Honor at Boskone, Boston; convention publishes *Unsilent Night* (NESFA Press) for the occasion; *Lycanthia* and *Delusion's Master* published by DAW; *Silver Metal Lover* published as original by Science Fiction Book Club (Nelson Doubleday); teleplay, "Sand," airs on *Blake's 7*.

1982 *Princess on a White Horse* published by Macmillan; *Death's Master, Cyrion*, and *Silver Metal Lover* published by DAW.

1983 *Sung in Shadow, Red as Blood*, and *Anackire* published by DAW; wins World Fantasy Award for "The Gorgon."

1984 *The Dragon Hoard* published by Ace; *Tamastara, or, The Indian Nights* published by DAW; *The Beautiful Biting Machine* published by Cheap Street; Guest of Honor at the World Fantasy Convention, Ottawa, Canada; wins World Fantasy Award for "Elle Est Troi (La Mort)."

1985 *Days of Grass* and *The Gorgon and Other Beastly Tales* published by DAW.

1986 *Dreams Light and Dark* (major retrospective collection) published by Arkham House; *Dark Castle, White Horse* (omnibus of *The Castle of the Dark* and *Prince on a White Horse*) and *Delirium's Mistress* published by DAW.

1987 *Night's Sorceries* published by DAW.

1988 Special "Tanith Lee issue" of *Weird Tales* published (Summer); *Madame Two Swords* published by Donald Grant; *The White Serpent* published by DAW; *The Book of the Damned* and *The Book of the Beast* published by Unwin Paperbacks (UK)

1989 *Women as Demons* (collection) published by Women's Press (UK); *Forests of the Night* published by Unwin Hyman (UK).

1990 *The Book Damned* and *The Book of the Beast* published by Overlook Press; *The Blood of Roses* published by Century Legend (UK).

1991 *Black Unicorn* published by Atheneum; *The Book of the Dead* published by Overlook Press; *Into Gold* published by Pulphouse.

1992 *Dark Dance* published by Macdonald (UK) and Dell; *Heart-Beast* published by Headline (UK).

1993 *Elephantasm* and *Nightshades* (collection) published by Headline (UK); *Personal Darkness* published by Little, Brown (UK); *The Book of the Mad* published by Overlook Press.

1994 *Darkness, I* published by Little, Brown (UK); *Eva Fairdeath* published by Headline (UK).

A TANITH LEE INTERVIEW

SCHWEITZER: What is the major appeal of out-and-out scary stories?

LEE: There is a lot in the world that frightens people, and the one way you can come to terms with it is by experiencing fear second-hand, when you know you can put the book away, or turn the television off, or walk out of the film if you have to. It's a form of practice for fear, because we all experience fear in our lives. We can't avoid it. If we go through it second-hand, we're practicing, and then we can face it if we have to. That's the education part. I also think people just like to be frightened because it gets the adrenalin going and gives them excitement they don't always have in their own lives.

SCHWEITZER: Is this entirely an emotional thing, or does it come in part from an intellectual appreciation of disconcerting reality?

LEE: It's a gut thing. People have always done it. The Greeks knew about it and called it "catharsis," going through a whole range of emotions, not only fear, but pain and sorrow and gladness. It's something we do instinctively. I'm intellectualizing about it, but we all do it instinctively.

SCHWEITZER: Do you scare yourself when writing?

LEE: Sometimes. Yes, it happens a lot. I give myself nightmares. There's a children's book called *The Castle of Dark*, which has a kind of vampire spirit which possesses a girl, and when I finally got the image, which appeared to me as most of my images do—it started as a picture in my mind, of how this thing was evolving from this girl's body like black smoke with two glowing eyes in it. I frightened the hell out of myself, and I slept all that night with a light on.

SCHWEITZER: Does it go away when you've written it?

LEE: Not necessarily. Sometimes when I write it, it stirs up the feeling again. But it does go eventually.

SCHWEITZER: What does the writer have to do in order to make fear come across to the reader? We've all read lots of horror stories that don't work. What makes the ones that work do so?

LEE: Good writing. The better your style is, the more you can put across. But you do get people who are lousy stylists but excellent at telling frightening stories, and you do get people who write exquisitely who are very bad storytellers. If you get a combination of the two, they instinctively know what they're doing. Also, your own reactions are a pretty good yardstick. If you scare the hell out of yourself, you are of course going to scare a few other people.

SCHWEITZER: A common problem—I think it comes in the backwash of Lovecraft—is that the writer spends the entire story building up to what the story is about. When he gets to what scares him, he stops. Does this make a story ineffective?

LEE: It depends what you want to do with a story. If you really just want to scare people, there's no reason you shouldn't stop. That is sometimes the most disturbing element. You get to the point of terror, and then you leave everybody with this apparently insoluble problem. Many really satisfying horror stories do more. I'm thinking of something that really scared me—*The Day of the Triffids*, by John Wyndham. I'm still scared of triffids. Admittedly, it's a novel and not a short story. There, he introduces the problem, and there are a number of searing climaxes, but eventually the characters come to terms with the problem and deal with it the best they can. At the end of the book you are left still with the terror, but with a working solution.

61

SCHWEITZER: It seems to me that the people who just build up to the story's premise are the same ones who would have written *Dracula* four chapters long, ending with the revelation that he's a vampire.

LEE: [*Laughs*] Not necessarily. No, I still think it's valid to end with that climax of terror, because it leaves a very nasty, frightening taste in the mouth. What do you *do*? But you're not told what to do. And if you want to, intellectually, you can go away and ask yourself what would you have done, how would you have handled that?

SCHWEITZER: What is the appeal vampires have for you?

LEE: I don't know. I've been asked this before. A lot of people are fascinated by vampires. I think it's probably a wish-fulfillment: how lovely to be slim and pale and flawless. It's a bit of a drag that you can't go out in the daylight, but I suppose one could overcome that. It's a bit of a drag that you can't *eat* except for one thing, but I suppose you could get used to it. And there are the lovely attributes that they have on the side, not being seen in mirrors, and so on. One either wants to use that because it's extremely romantic in a couple of ways, or one wants to examine it and think, "Well is it true, and if it is true, why?" Which is basically a scientific approach. And if it isn't true, let's get rid of it. They're just *very* appealing. They're always beautiful—not so much nowadays, but they always used to be *desperately* elegant. I mean, black silk and white lace and blood-red rings and so on.

SCHWEITZER: When you were a child, did you ever want to grow up and be a vampire? For a while, though I knew it to be impossible, I thought it would be very nice.

LEE: Not consciously, but I think I must have done it unconsciously. I think I wanted to have vampires among my friends, but even then I had a sort of suspicion that what I liked doing best was writing. I guess it would suit my lifestyle to be a vampire. But how do you know I haven't grown up to be a vampire? This could all be a ruse.

SCHWEITZER: Actually, Stoker's Dracula did come out in broad daylight. Now, I haven't seen you turn into a bat or a wolf, but he couldn't use any of his powers in broad daylight. He could only do that at night. So I'm beginning to have suspicions.

LEE: [*Laughs*] Well, stick around. You might see something flapping over the Sheraton later...

SCHWEITZER: How often do you start something as a horror story and it comes out funny, either deliberately or not?

LEE: They usually tell me what they want to be. But there was a story called "The Third Horseman" that I sold to *Weirdbook* [no. 14]. It was a vampire story. Now, I originally wrote this story when I was very young indeed, and when I wrote it, it was funny—*extremely* funny—and very ironical. When I came to write it again, because I knew I liked the story more than I liked the format, though I must say it amused me, it came out as one of the most depressing and, I think, horrible stories I've ever written. But, of course, the thing with horror is that you've only got to tilt your perceptions very slightly and it can be screamingly funny. Triffids, for example, stumbling about clumsily. It could be hilarious.

SCHWEITZER: Is this nervous laughter, or a sense of the absurd?

LEE: I think it's a sense of the absurd. But people do giggle when they're afraid. Well, consider Roman Polanski's *Dance of the Vampires* [also known as *Fearless Vampire Killers*], which is deliciously funny, and it manages to be terribly frightening and terribly scary in several places, *very* depressing at the end, while being funny as well, which is very clever. It also makes a kind of definitive statement about vampires. It's very sensible in the way it deals with them. They're logical. It is very funny, so I suppose you could have a horror story that was screamingly funny and terrifying as well. Why not?

SCHWEITZER: What are your writing methods like? Do you just sit down and do it, or outline?

LEE: I did do an outline a couple of times, but it's very unusual. I always feel that the story is there. It's a matter of picking it up on the receiver, and keeping at it until I've got it all, as if it has a transmitter somewhere. Now, maybe it has, and I am picking it up, but I just let it come, and I write it, and the characters tell me plots they think they want to do. Sometimes they have to be checked a little bit. They do terrible things like getting killed when I don't expect them to, or not getting killed when they really ought to. They tell me. The outline's there, but I haven't written it. It's somewhere floating in the atmosphere.

SCHWEITZER: Do you think that your subconscious writes the story and then lets it surface?

LEE: No, I don't think it's my subconscious. I think my subconscious sometimes works out problems in plot that I'm finding difficult. Sometimes I have to hammer them out with blood, sweat, and tears, stamping around my workroom talking to myself, but I've become convinced it isn't me. Now that's probably quite wrong, but it does feel like it's something coming in, like radio waves floating in the atmosphere. It's almost as if I'm picking those up. I think it's probably fragments that one's got from various things, and perhaps race memories, but I don't think it can be just the subconscious, no.

SCHWEITZER: Do you mean race memories in the classical sense?

LEE: I mean race memories. After all, we're all built of all these genes in little bits and pieces that come through to us from the very beginning of our ancestry, and it seems to me quite logical that some of those genes can carry recollections. Some people are more susceptible to it than others, which means one's seen a hell of a lot of things, the genes have, and if they can pass it on to the brain, one could pick it up, and amalgamate a bit here and a bit there, and you'd have a story and a set of characters.

SCHWEITZER: Do you ever write from dreams, or base stories strongly on dreams?

LEE: I have done a couple things, one short story which I can't recall, strangely enough, but I know I did it, and it was based solely on a dream. What usually happens is that when I'm writing, I sometimes have dreams which are loosely related to what I'm writing. I will then incorporate perhaps one or a couple of those dreams in the book, as dreams, tailoring them to fit the way the characters work. I've done that on several occasions.

SCHWEITZER: Are you influenced by other writers, those you once took as models, for instance?

LEE: I'm influenced by everybody. I'm influenced by everything I see, everything I read, every rumor I pick up, every person I meet. They all influence me, and no one more than another. But of course I'm influenced, because I'm influenced by everything.

SCHWEITZER: When you were younger, did you ever have a writer who was sort of an idol, to be emulated?

LEE: Not to be emulated. Of course, I'm quite sure that if you're madly in love with a particular writer, you probably do pick up a few things. I would never set out to emulate somebody even if I admired them desperately, because we're all different, and they're doing something that is not what I'm doing. This doesn't stop me from being madly in love with them.

SCHWEITZER: Is there an element of wish-fulfillment in your fiction?

LEE: [I once did a] novel set in a parallel Renaissance Italy that is full of wonderful clothes, wonderful views, wonderful sword fights, and lots of blood and mayhem. Its manuscript title was *Sung in the Shadow of Night*. I'd love to have been an agile sword fighter. I probably was sometime.

SCHWEITZER: In a previous incarnation?

LEE: Well, how else?

SCHWEITZER: Do you have any serious occult beliefs?

LEE: No, not really. I have practiced a very minor form of witchcraft which is based on willpower, self-fulfillment, and self-desire, and positive thinking, and sometimes it's worked very well, and I think it's possible that we all have the ability to do it. It interests me, but I don't know an awful lot about it.

SCHWEITZER: It does seem to me that all of us are believers in the supernatural under the skin, and this may be the appeal of such fiction. Consciously, we don't believe it, but subconsciously we do. We're all superstitious, whether we admit it or not.

LEE: You see, I believe in it consciously, because I think there are these powers around in ourselves, mainly, which are responsible for an awful lot of the weird things that happen to us and to other people. Certainly, I'm extremely superstitious. I would never walk under a ladder because I found that if I did walk under a ladder, something pretty horrible would happen. Now, I believe that was me, because I had picked up the superstition and I was afraid it would happen, and I partly made it happen. I got myself into situations in which I was nervous, where they happened, or my will—which is quite strong—was influencing things and they turned out badly. Then I found out that if you walk under a ladder and cross your fingers and wish for something, it negates the ill luck and you have a very good chance of getting your wish to come true. In fact, the very first time I did it, I had just written to DAW Books, and said, "Would you be interested in seeing a synopsis of my novel?" And they said, "Yes." Now, I still believe that it was that wish under that ladder that did that.

SCHWEITZER: I had an experience where a witch offered to cast a spell for me. She said, "Anything you want." So I said, "Make my next story sell." So she did, and it almost did. The only problem was...I was supposed to take a lavender-scented bath at midnight while burning a green candle, and I declined to do this. So, while the story was accepted, the anthology never came out, and I've had this curse ever since.

LEE: Those things that witches use, they're focusing agents. This is the primary importance to all those things that witches use that are accessories to witchcraft. They are means of focusing and they are means of proving to yourself that you are really doing that thing. Had you taken the lavender-scented bath—Oh, how lovely!—while burning the green candle, however ridiculous you felt, and however ridiculous you smelled afterwards, you would have had it firmly fixed in your mind that you'd done it. That activates your willpower. I guess the lady knew you wouldn't do it, so she was working for you. She may have sensed, because she'd have to be fairly sensitive if she's a witch, that you hadn't done it, and that would help negate her power. So, you had the beneficial side working for you, but you negated it. I think you should duplicate those conditions sometime, and *do* it again, and see what happens.

SCHWEITZER: The manuscript was already in the mail, so how would my willpower have mattered at all? It should have been the editor's that mattered.

LEE: Do you mean it was in the mail coming back to you or going out?

SCHWEITZER: It was going out.

LEE: But he hadn't seen it yet?

SCHWEITZER: I don't think he had.

LEE: That's exactly it. What you were doing, in fact, was extending your willpower because you wanted him to publish it. I would imagine that if you were a really terrible writer and had written a really awful manuscript, it probably would not help, but assuming you have a good manuscript, one does need luck. One does need timing. It's very hard to guess at timing. So you're throwing a protective lasso around that work. You're putting a ring of light around it, saying, "I've done this thing. I have perpetrated these acts." They bolster it. So when he gets it, he feels that crackle of electricity, and it probably does influence him. Do you realize that all over this country people will now be taking lavender baths and burning green candles and we'll have a whole pile of stories being published?

SCHWEITZER: I suspect that the backfiring of this had wide-reaching consequences. The editor in question was Lin Carter, and the anthology would have come after what turned out to be the last anthology in the "Ballantine Adult Fantasy" series. Ever after I've had this history of selling to people who go out of business.

LEE: You're going to be so popular. [*Laughs*] You have a lot to answer for. What can I say? That's terrifying.

SCHWEITZER: I hope I'm not the Typhoid Mary of publishing. Thank you, Ms. Lee.

A SELECT SECONDARY BIBLIOGRAPHY ON TANITH LEE

Collings, Michael R. "Words and Worlds: The Creation of a Fantasy Universe in Zelazny, Lee, and Anthony," in *The Scope of the Fantastic*, edited by Robert A. Collins and Hazel D. Pierce. Westport, CT: Greenwood Press, 1985, p. 173-182.

Garratt, Peter. "Unstoppable Fate: Tanith Lee Interview," in *Interzone* no. 64 (October 1992): 23-25.

Gasser, Larry W. "Feminism and Tanith Lee's *The Birthgrave*," in Harbringer 1 (Spring 1976): 5-7.

Hardesty, W. H. III. "The Birthgrave Trilogy," in *Survey of Modern Fantasy Literature*, edited by Frank N. Magill. Englewood Cliffs, NJ: Salem Press, 1983, Vol. 1, p. 116-121.

Hardesty, W. H. III. "*Volkavaar*," in *Survey of Modern Fantasy Literature*, edited by Frank N. Magill. Englewood Cliffs, NJ: Salem Press, 1983, Vol. 4, p. 2036-2038.

Heldreth, Lillian M. "Author Profile: Tanith Lee," in *Science Fiction & Fantasy Book Review Annual 1990*, edited by Robert A. Collins and Robert Latham. Westport, CT: Greenwood Press, 1991, p. 61-70.

Heldreth, Lillian M. "Tanith Lee's Werewolves Within: Reversals of Gothic Tradition," in *Journal of the Fantastic in the Arts* 2 (Spring 1989): 25-14.

"Many Faces of Tanith Lee," in *Locus* 16 (November 1983): 4.

Perdone, Kitty. "Blood Sisters," in *Midnight Graffiti* 4 (Fall 1989): 46-50.

"Tanith Lee," in *Contemporary Literary Criticism, Volume 46*. Detroit: Gale Research Co., 1988, p. 230-234.

"Tanish Lee: A Selected Bibliography," in *Weird Tales* 50 (Summer 1988): 45.

Waggoner, Diana. "Tanith Lee," in *Supernatural Fiction Writers*, edited by E. F. Bleiler. New York: Charles Scribner's Sons, 1985, p. 1053-1058.

Watson, Christine. "The Master Books," in *Survey of Modern Fantasy Literature*, edited by Frank N. Magill. Englewood Cliffs, NJ: Salem Press, 1983, Vol. 2, p. 988-992.

Wollheim, Donald A. "Profile: Tanith Lee," in *Weird Tales* 50 (Summer 1988): 43-44.

VI.

THOMAS LIGOTTI

A Thomas Ligotti Chronology

1953   Thomas Ligotti born in Detroit, Michigan.

1971   Graduates from Grosse Pointe North High School.

1975   Receives B.A. degree in English from Wayne State University (Detroit).

1979   Joins the Literary Criticism Division of Gale Research Company (and continues to work there to date).

1981   First published story, "The Chymist," in *Nyctalops* no. 16 (March); "Allan & Adelaide: An Arabesque" published in *Fantasy Macabre* no. 2 (April); "Les Fleurs" published in *Dark Horizons: The Journal of the British Fantasy Society* no. 23 (Summer).

1982   "The Frolic" published in *Fantasy Tales* no. 9 (Spring); "Drink to Me Only with Labyrinthine Eyes" published in *Nyctalops* no. 17 (June); "Dream of a Mannikin, or the Third Person," published in *Eldritch Tales* no. 9.

1985   First edition of *Songs of a Dead Dreamer* (collection) published by Silver Scarab Press in an edition of 300 copies.

1986   "Masquerade of a Dead Sword" published in *Heroic Visions II*, edited by Jessica Amanda Salmonson (DAW); "The Lost Art of Twilight" published in *Dark Horizons* no. 30 (Summer).

1988   "Alice's Last Adventure" (revised version of story published in Silver Scarab Press edition of *Songs of a Dead Dreamer*) published in *Prime Evil*, edited by Douglas Winter (New American Library), an extremely prestigious anthology containing new stories by Stephen King, Clive Barker, Peter Straub, etc.; special "Thomas Ligotti issue" of *Dagon* (no. 22/23) published.

1989   Expanded edition of *Songs of a Dead Dreamer* published by Robinson (UK), reprinted in the U.S. by Carroll & Graf, 1990; special "Thomas Ligotti issue" of *Crypt of Cthulhu* (no. 68) published, Hallowmas (contains ten stories or prose poems by Ligotti, most of them reprints but hitherto uncollected).

1990 "The Last Feast of Harlequin" published in *The Magazine of Fantasy & Science Fiction* (April); "The Lost Art of Twilight" reprinted in *Weird Tales* no. 297 (Summer).

1991 *Grimscribe, His Lives and Works* (collection) published simultaneously by Robinson (UK) and Carroll and Graf (USA); "The Last Feast of Harlequin" is a finalist for the World Fantasy Award for Best Short Fiction. Special "Thomas Ligotti issue" of *Weird Tales* (no. 303) published (Winter 1991/92).

1992 Winter/Spring issue of *Tekeli-Li!: Journal of Terror* (no. 4) features a Thomas Ligotti section; *Grimscribe, His Lives and Works* is a finalist for the World Fantasy Award for Best Collection.

1994 *Noctuary* (collection) published simultaneously by Robinson (UK) and Carroll & Graf (USA).

A Thomas Ligotti Interview

SCHWEITZER: Tom, your career has followed quite a different trajectory from that of most writers. You have achieved considerable prominence *without* the traditional reliance on novels, or even publication in many major outlets. You seem to be one of the very few writers to become genuinely famous through the small press. Then you jump from special Ligotti issues of *Crypt of Cthulhu* and *Dagon* to having your collection, *Songs of a Dead Dreamer*, published by a mainstream house, Carroll & Graf. I'm impressed, and so, I am sure, are quite a lot of other people. What's your secret?

LIGOTTI: I don't see my situation as unprecedented by any means, especially when you consider the case of someone like T. E. D. Klein, who became a major presence in weird fiction-land after the publication of only a few stories. Or Ramsey Campbell, who could have dropped dead after publishing *Demons by Daylight* and still loomed large in the post-Lovecraft era of supernatural horror writing.

Maybe my perspective is a bit insular, but I find it difficult to imagine myself as approaching the stature of early Klein or Campbell, and in any case psychologically unprofitable to do so. Nevertheless, I do feel fortunate in gaining the attention of some hardcore fanatics of horror tales, from Harry O. Morris, who illustrated and published the original, limited-run Silver Scarab Press edition of *Songs of a Dead Dreamer*, to editors and writers like Douglas Winter, Robert Price, Ramsey Campbell, Stefan Dziemianowicz, Mike Ashley, and some guy named Darrell Schweitzer.

SCHWEITZER: Then where do you fit into the context of weird literature, or literature in general, both as a writer and as a reader?

LIGOTTI: For my part, I suppose that I managed to find a certain audience in readers who still take seriously, as I do—writers like Poe and Lovecraft, as well as a great many other writers whose works are related to the supernatural genre without being strictly demarcated by its "conventions." This latter group forms a gallery of eccentric, for the most part grim-minded, and occasionally demented figures in world literature, from Aloysius Bertrand to the late nineteenth-century decadents to early twentieth-century writers like Georg Trakl and Bruno Schulz, and more recent masters of the postmodern nightmare, including Samuel Beckett, Dino Buzzati, and Jorge Luis Borges.

In general, my reading tends toward authors of a morbid, negative type. These are really the ones who have perpetuated the tradition of horror in literature, because their works reveal the outrageously strange and terrible as integral to existence, a fascinating turbulence never to be quelled, and not simply a momentary or isolated aberration succeeded by reconciliation with the world, or even its affirmation. Lately I've been reading the melancholy aphorisms of Logan Pearsall Smith and the novels, which are more properly described as multi-hundred-page monologues, of Thomas Bernhard.

SCHWEITZER: What got you started writing and when?

LIGOTTI: I started writing outside of school assignments, that is about my third year of college. I found the required writing that I was doing to be very stimulating: it made me high, or at least distracted me from my chronic anxiety, and I wanted to do more of it. This was very like the experience I had with reading—I had read only a few books before college—only more intense. I was very much aware that for me both reading and writing were practiced as a form of escapism, but in a paradoxical way, since I usually escaped *into* a sort of imaginary hell. Perhaps you might call this a *confrontational* escapism.

SCHWEITZER: For all your success, you can't possibly be earning a living from short stories and a single collection, no matter how prestigiously it may be published. So, what else do you do?

LIGOTTI: I've earned my living for the past fifteen years doing editorial work for a reference book company in Detroit called Gale Research. I work in the literary criticism division of the company, which produces several series of books that reprint selected commentary on authors from antiquity to the present day. Many, if not most of the entries we compile represent the first, and probably only, time that anyone has gathered English-language criticism on that author. Where else can you find an assemblage of critical writings on the works of Hanns Heinz Ewers, not to mention a picture of the scarred mug of horror literature's favorite Nazi apologist?

SCHWEITZER: Let's talk about the influence of Lovecraft on your work. It's virtually impossible to come into this field without falling under the shadow of HPL at some point, and I should think it would be completely impossible to do so in the pages of *Nyctalops*, which is where many readers first encountered you. Yet your stories only resemble Lovecraft's in the most tenuous manner, in that you too seem to depict a bleak and uncertain universe in which human assumptions don't apply very far. But the more overt Lovecraftisms, from the adjectives to the tentacular Things from Beyond, are conspicuously absent.

LIGOTTI: I think your characterization of Lovecraft's literary universe as "bleak and uncertain" is accurate enough, especially with respect to works like "The Music of Erich Zann" and "The Colour Out of Space." The more science-fictional stories like "At the Mountains of Madness" and "The Shadow Out of Time" are arguably another matter, since they outline metaphysical schemes that are not at all uncertain, perhaps even too simplistic and comprehensible, and certainly depict a universe that is no less "grand" and no more bleak than those of most religious and myth systems. What is missing in Lovecraft are the human relationships that serve as the focus and prime impetus of almost all fiction, horror and otherwise. While such relationships may serve as either a source of fear or a safety net, the bottom line is that they divert attention from the macrocosmic mysteries which may be exalting or dreadful or both, depending on one's mood; but these cosmic mysteries never offer the kind of hope and potential consolation that lurks behind the pages of practically all horror fiction since its beginnings in the gothic novel. So, yes, I would agree that my stories could be called Lovecraftian in having a fairly steady view of the bleak and uncertain cosmos.

SCHWEITZER: You seem to differ from Lovecraft in your lack of scientific realism. Remember how HPL used to say that a story should be put together with all the care of a thorough-going hoax? Yours seem to be more like disturbing dreams. I don't see the realist-hoaxer in you. So, is this a partial rejection of the Lovecraftian method, or just a difference in sensibilities?

LIGOTTI: As far as Lovecraft's fictional method of "scientific realism" is concerned, I can't believe that Lovecraft ever looked back on any of his works and considered them to be successful realism, though at certain points in his career there were stories partly based on the Poe-instigated intention of pulling off a literary hoax, a strategy Poe himself almost never employed in his horror tales.

Lovecraft always veered off into a highly unrealistic, as well as highly poetic style. He was at his worst when he tried to be "convincing" in the manner derived from the late nineteenth-century realist-naturalist writers. And of course, toward the end of his life Lovecraft expressed in his letters quite a bit of confusion concerning the most effective approach to weird fiction, feeling that with few exceptions he had failed to capture in literary form his most powerful sensations and visions. It's no news that he always feared that his exposure to the stories in *Weird Tales* would pervert his ideals and methods as a horror writer, and to an extent this fear seems to have been realized.

SCHWEITZER: What do you think a good horror story should be? Should it raise shrieks, or is disquiet enough?

LIGOTTI: I can only attempt an answer by stating my biases regarding what a horror story should *not* be. This is very risky, because there are so many impurities in any form of literature, and in fact the essential interest of literature itself may well depend on the impure concoction of the artistic use of language and the human experience that for the most part motivates literary language. If literature as a whole is largely founded on impurity, how can any specialized form such as the horror tale aspire to purity, especially when so many of the impurities are the result of an often quite interesting cross-pollination with other literary forms? It can't, of course; it can only fight the same losing battle of every other human endeavor. This battle, most of all, is against the popular *pull* of the horror genre. As Poe rightly declared, "Terror is not of Germany" or the United States "but of the soul." And while that soul may be strolling down the streets of San Francisco or the sidewalks of New York, it ultimately paces in isolation in a realm all its own, a realm that is as claustrophobic as a nightmare and as expansive as...well, you get the idea. No doubt any form of writing is popular within a certain circle, but if that circle is too wide it remains one-dimensional, lying flat on the earth rather than spinning into a sphere that moves through stranger dimensions.

SCHWEITZER: I don't really understand what you mean by the "impure concoction of the artistic use of language and the human experience that motivates literary language" and forms the essential interest of literature. Do you mean that if somehow we were able to write with absolute and utter clarity and understand the impulses and experiences that went into the writing just as absolutely and clearly, there would be no fruitful ambiguity left and therefore no further basis for literature?

LIGOTTI: I probably over-expressed myself. Very simply, I'm referring to the possibility that the fascination of reading may derive neither from the subject portrayed nor from the language that portrays it, but from the relationship between the two; that is, a relationship in which literary language does not communicate subject matter but rather *processes* it, a debased intercourse between life and art, the offspring of which is a recombined creature born of experience and expression. A unique little bastard.

SCHWEITZER: To put it another way, then, what do you most admire about the stories you do admire?

LIGOTTI: The technique of delineating a condition of pervasive strangeness and unease is the approach I most admire in horror fiction, and the one that supports the haunting memorableness of such tales as Algernon Blackwood's "The Willows" and Lovecraft's "The Colour Out of Space." Like electroshock therapy, sudden or violent frights of the "pop-up" type may make a strong momentary impression, but overall the effect is to annihilate the emotion and the consciousness that are crucial for a really profound sense of horror, the purest possible sense of horror.

SCHWEITZER: You also write horror fiction *about* horror fiction. Surely that is a delicate act to pull off. What are the strengths and limitations of this approach?

LIGOTTI: The nature of horror fiction is a subject like any other, though one that probably interests a relatively small faction of the horror-reading public. Then again, the one knowable trait shared by all readers of horror fiction is that they read horror fiction, so why shouldn't they be interested? I imagine that most readers, whatever their taste in fiction, end up reading the same basic story told in the same basic style until the day they die.

SCHWEITZER: The *pull* of horror literature, as I see it, is not toward self-examination of the form, but in the direction of the Stephen King or Dean Koontz type of story, which is easily understood and completely within the reader's frame of everyday reference, *and* very emotionally compelling. In other words, make 'em laugh, make 'em cry, rip their hearts out, but make sure you do it in Suburbia, USA, 1994. My guess is that King has such wide appeal not so much for his monsters as for his ability to depict fathers and sons (and husbands and wives) drawn together by crisis. Common emotions, honestly and clearly presented. That's the way to multi-millionaire superstardom.

LIGOTTI: Your analysis could be extended to bestselling fiction in general. The works that enjoy the most success in the marketplace are naturally those that are the most accessible to the greatest number of people. Hence, Beckett's big hit is *Waiting for Godot*, which is relatively easy to *get* when contrasted with just about any of his other works. Poe is most celebrated for his detective stories and holds an honored place in that genre, but to contemporary readers of horror fiction he's practically invisible, judging from the minimal attention his works receive in horrorzines and the infrequency with which his name arises in interviews with horror writers of today. Why should this be the case? Because his horror stories, when placed beside his detective stories, are poetic and obscure. Most readers have little patience or sympathy with such works. This is perfectly understandable. I'm very much this way when it comes to movies. With few exceptions, I don't care for artistically ambitious, serious films and can only tolerate action extravaganzas or adaptations of blockbuster horror novels.

SCHWEITZER: How about something more about yourself? Did you have an upbringing which directed you toward writing horror fiction?

LIGOTTI: Almost certainly, but it's difficult to say just how. For instance, when I was two years old I was operated on for an internal rupture. Now, Bram Stoker also underwent surgery as an infant and there's an article that asserts the effect of this early "surgical trauma" on his writings. I'm told that I was quite alert and cheerful throughout this ordeal, including the truss-wearing aftermath, but I've noticed in the last couple of years that a disproportionate number of my tales feature doctors of one sort or another. But who really knows?

Another "for-instance": I was a Catholic until I was eighteen years old, when I unloaded all of the doctrines, but almost none of the fearful superstition, of a gothically devout childhood and youth. This superstitiousness was abetted in a small way by an old woman who used to babysit me and my two younger brothers. Her name was Mrs. Rinaldi and she specialized in telling religious cautionary tales. One of them particularly impressed me. It was about a poor woman who kept finding her laundry pulled from the clothesline outside her house and trampled in the dirt. She thought the Devil was doing this deed when actually it was just the neighborhood kids. In her irrational state of exasperation, she offered to give the Devil anything if he would allow her a clean batch of clothes. Well, the Devil takes care of the pranksters, all right, and then demands the woman fulfill her part of the bargain by turning over to him her infant son, which she has no choice but to do. Years later the son, who is now a full-grown demon, pays a visit to his mother to show her what he has done to him. There's something very captivating about this atrociously senseless tale. I was reminded of it recently in reading a collection of Eskimo folktales. What nightmares those people dreamed up! *Very* nice.

Probably the most important factor in my taking interest in writing fiction in general was the emotional breakdown I alluded to earlier. This occurred in August 1970, following intense use of drugs and booze, though these intoxicants served only as a catalyst for a fate that my high-strung and mood-swinging self would have encountered at some point. Before that time, I had no interest in reading or writing, though I tested well in these subjects; afterward, they became the only ways I could alter my state of mind without fear, at least without *extreme* fear, of losing my grip entirely. My condition is called agoraphobia; it's part hereditary, and I continue to experience its symptoms, including panic attacks and a general sense of unreality.

SCHWEITZER: Did you ever have any other plans for your life, other than to be a writer?

LIGOTTI: No. Having an identity as a horror writer is about the closest thing I've come to distinctly *doing* anything with my life. When I was a kid I had a vague ambition to be a baseball player, then a rock-and-roll musician. I still fool around with electric guitar privately, but there's not much to be said for my musical ability. Recreationally, I also attend the local harness-race tracks regularly with my younger brother, who introduced me to the manic-depressive pleasures of this pastime and who is the dedicatee of my second collection of horror stories. You want to know terror? Try waiting for the results of a photo-finish between the horse you loaded up on and some other hayburner.

SCHWEITZER: What are you working on for the near future? While we're at it, do you have any thoughts on where your future is as a horror writer?

LIGOTTI: It's hard to say. I'd like to write more than I have in the past few years, but I'm often too distracted or lack the energy to do anything about it. This is probably just as well. My recent collection, *Grimscribe: His Lives and Works*, includes stories that are all told from the first-person anonymous point of view, and may be looked upon as chronicles of an epicure or victim of the weird.

SCHWEITZER: Thanks, Tom.

A SELECT SECONDARY BIBLIOGRAPHY ON THOMAS LIGOTTI

Ashley, Mike. "The Knave of Darkness, The Evolution of Horror in the Fiction of Thomas Ligotti," in *Dagon* no. 22/23 (September/December 1988).

Dziemianowicz, Stefan R. "Anecdotes of Some Obscure Hell: An Appreciation of Thomas Ligotti," in *Tekeli-Li!: Journal of Terror* no. 4 (Winter/Spring 1992).

Dziemianowicz, Stefan R. "Author Profile: Thomas Ligotti," in *Science Fiction & Fantasy Book Review Annual 1990*, edited by Robert A. Collins and Robert Latham. Westport, CT: Greenwood Press, 1991, p. 109-119.

Dziemianowicz, Stefan R. "Nothing Is What It Seems to Be: Thomas Ligotti's Assault on Certainty," in *Dagon* no. 22/23 (September/December 1988).

Frenschkowski, Marco. "Über Thomas Ligotti," in *Quarber Merkur* 29 (December 1991): 61-64/

Joshi, S. T. "Thomas Ligotti: The Escape from Life," in *The Modern Weird Tale*. Austin, TX: University of Texas Press. (Forthcoming).

MacCulloch, Simon. "'The Lost Art of Twilight': Two Aspects of the Vampire," in *Dagon* no. 22/23 (September/December 1988).

Morris, Christine. "Beyond Dualism: An Appreciation of the Writing of Thomas Ligotti," in *Dagon* no. 22/23 (September/December 1988).

Morris. Harry O. Jr. "Electro-Dynamics for the Beginner: An Appreciation of Thomas Ligotti," in *Tekeli-Li!: Journal of Terror* no. 4 (Winter/Spring 1992).

Price, Robert M. "The Mystagogue, the Gnostic Quest, the Secret Book," in *Dagon* no. 22/23 (September/December 1988).

Price, Robert M. "Thomas Ligotti's Gnostic Quest," in *Studies in Weird Fiction* no. 9 (Spring 1991).

VII.

BRIAN LUMLEY

A BRIAN LUMLEY CHRONOLOGY

1937   Brian Lumley born in the coal-mining village of Hodern, County Durham.

1958   Lumley called to national service, assigned to Royal Military Police. In military service for twenty-two years, with much travel, including Berlin and Cyprus, and acting as quartermaster of Edinburgh Castle. First reads Lovecraft in late '50s.

1968   First published story, "The Cyprus Shell," appears in August Derleth's magazine, *The Arkham Collector*.

1971   *The Caller of the Black* published by Arkham House.

1974   *Beneath the Moors* published by Arkham House. *The Burrowers Beneath* published by DAW (reprinted in hardcover by Ganley, 1988).

1975   *The Transition of Titus Crow* published by DAW (reprinted in hardcover by Ganley, 1992).

1977   *The Horror at Oakdeene and Others* published by Arkham House.

1978   *The Clock of Dreams* and *The Spawn of the Winds* published by Jove.

1979   *In the Moons of Borea* published by Jove.

1981   Lumley leaves military service. Becomes a full-time writer. *Khai of Ancient Khem* published by Jove.

1984   *Psychosphere* and *Psychomech* published in UK by Grafton. Special "Brian Lumley issue" of *Crypt of Cthulhu* published (Candlemas). *The Return of the Deep Ones* serialized in *Fantasy Book*. *The House of Cthulhu and Other Tales of the Primal Land* published by W. Paul Ganley.

1985   *Psychamok* published by Grafton.

1986   *Necroscope* published in UK (American edition, Tor 1988). *Hero of Dreams* published by Ganley. *Ship of Dreams* published by Ganley.

1987   *Demogorgon* published in UK (American edition, Tor, 1992). *Mad Moon of Dreams* and *The Complete Crow* published by Ganley.

1988   "Fruiting Bodies" published in *Weird Tales* no. 291 (Summer). *Necroscope II: Vamphyri!* published in UK (American edition, Tor, 1989).

1989   *Necroscope III: The Source* published by Tor. *Elysia, The Coming of Cthulhu* published by Ganley. "Fruiting Bodies" wins the British Fantasy Award for Best Short Story. Special "Brian Lumley issue" of *Weird Tales* published (no. 295, Winter 1989/90).

1990   Excerpt from *Necroscope III: The Source* wins award from *Fear* magazine. *The House of Doors* published by Tor. *Necroscope IV: Deadspeak* published by Tor.

1991   *Necroscope V: Deadspawn* published by Tor. *The Complete Khash, Volume One: Never a Backward Glance* published by Ganley.

1992   *Iced on Aran and Other Dream Quests* published by Ganley. *Blood Brothers* published by Tor.

1993   *The Last Aerie* published by Tor. *Fruiting Bodies and Other Fungi* published by Tor.

1994   *Return of the Deep Ones and Other Mythos Tales* published by Roc (UK).

A Brian Lumley Interview

SCHWEITZER: What sort of writer do you think you would have been if you had never discovered Lovecraft?

LUMLEY: It may be that I would never have tried my hand at it. Lovecraft had a style of writing that attracted me greatly, perhaps because I'm English. Perhaps the fact that he was an Anglophile came through in his writing. Certainly his work, while unique, reminded me more of the old English school of macabre writers than anything else I had come across. I suppose the germ of a scrivener in all of us who turn out to be authors has to have an inspiration, a moment when it suddenly dawns: "Wow! I *have* to write." For me, Lovecraft was that inspiration. If I hadn't read his stuff, I don't suppose I would have written a word.

SCHWEITZER: When did you read him?

LUMLEY: The first Mythos story I remember reading was Robert Bloch's "Notebook Found in a Deserted House." That was the one that set me off, not writing, but searching. I found Lovecraft's early paperback, *Cry Horror*, in Germany some seven or eight years later. I read that, realized that there were a lot more stories in the same vein—jugular, as Bloch might say—following which I couldn't get enough of the stuff. I had to track it all down.

SCHWEITZER: At what stage of your life was this?

LUMLEY: Discovering Lovecraft came in about 1951. In about 1959, I read the majority of Lovecraft's work. Wanting to be a writer, well, as a *hobby*: this came right at the beginning, from finding Lovecraft and wanting to write in that vein. That's when that happened. As for wanting to do it professionally: that wasn't really the case until about 1976, would you believe, long after I'd had books published! It wasn't my business. My business was being a soldier. It was only when the end of the army loomed and the bread line seemed to be there in the corner of my eye that I decided to turn the pen into a regular ploughshare, plant some corn, and get some bread out of this thing.

SCHWEITZER: I assume you got a great deal of encouragement from August Derleth before that.

LUMLEY: If I look back now and read August Derleth's letters to me and try to remember the ones I wrote back to him...it's difficult. Now, I would say that I didn't rely on his advice a lot, that my stories weren't changed a lot, that I would have done what I did anyway. But I simply can't be sure. As a beginning writer, any beginning writer is a novice, I suppose that I harkened to a man I didn't know, had never seen, had never met, had never spoken to on the phone—I do believe that I did speak to him on the phone on one or two occasions, but I honestly can remember nothing about them—and he did, I suppose, have an influence. But all to the good. I'm told by various people different stories about Derleth. I can never remember him being thoroughly discouraging in any way, in respect to my stories. That's not to say he didn't tell me a few of them were no good. He did, and the ones he said that about *were* no good!

SCHWEITZER: Is your interest still primarily in writing in the Lovecraft vein?

LUMLEY: My interest *was* in that vein. If you mean "against Lovecraft's background," yes, I've always enjoyed that. I've no doubt that there will be future stories set against the Lovecraft background. But I rarely considered that I was writing Lovecraft pastiches. Of course, if you *imitate* someone's style, it comes out sounding like pastiche. I never intended that. Anybody who has read *Heggopian* or *Born of the Wind* or *The Return of the Deep Ones* will realize that there is stuff in there that Lovecraft would never have done. It's done against his background, but not in his style. However much it may sound Lovecraftian, there is stuff he wouldn't have done. Simply, I rarely considered that I was writing Lovecraftian pastiches. What I was wanting to do was use the Mythos lore, which had been borrowed from time and time again. I was interested mainly in tacking some of my own ideas onto the Cthulhu Mythos.

SCHWEITZER: There's been a lot of talk in Lovecraftian criticism these days to the effect that Derleth profoundly changed the Cthulhu Mythos, so that it's very un-Lovecraftian presently. Do you agree? What is your conception of the Mythos?

LUMLEY: Yes, he did change it and shouldn't have. That way I'd have been able to do a much better job of it. If I could go back and start again, I'd ignore all he'd done. And by now, a lot more people would be condemning me and not him! My conception of the Cthulhu Mythos is a series of stories set against a more-or-less homogeneous background, in which certain myths, legends, come through and are repeated or reiterated by the addition, occasionally, of some extra information, by the expansion of concepts which really needed expanding upon—which might be only hinted at in earlier stories, but developed into a full-fledged concept in later stories—which is unified by a series of locations and dates of world-shaking events, such as the raising of R'lyeh, and which centers around, necessarily, the mind and concepts of its creator, Lovecraft. So, to stray too far from the Lovecraft focus is to bend the rules too far.

But the Mythos can be used in as many different ways as that many writers can conceive of. People have put it to me: "Don't you think you've taken it too far? Don't you think you've taken the rise out of it?" No, I don't. Now, if people don't want to accept my ideas, fine, go ahead, write a different sort of story. Do it a different way. I won't complain at all. The Mythos is too expansive; too much has been written about it, too many variants have appeared, for *anyone* now to start screaming about which is the real one. Of course, you can stop it all dead, remove the whole thing, leave only Lovecraft's original skeleton. But if you do that, how many fans will never get anywhere near a fantasy convention? How many would-be writers will never write? How much interest will be lost forever? What of the really good stories which would then never be written? Do it the way some people would, and the Mythos would stagnate. You *cannot* keep reading "The Dunwich Horror" and "The Call of Cthulhu" over and over again, unless you happen to be some *nut* who can't read anything else. If you want stagnation, that's the way you can do it. That way, you can go to a three-monthly meeting of the local crazy bunch and listen to them exemplify Lovecraft and deify him to the end of time. Or, you can sit down with a decent book or story now and then and read a *good* one.

Fan fiction? There'll always be fan fiction. Some of the world's best writers were once fans. I've got nothing against them doing it and writing their own fiction. And if you've got to start somewhere, why not start in the Mythos, where so many others have started? But kill it off? No, I don't believe in that at all. I don't think stagnation should be allowed to occur. The people who would have it that way are already stagnant.

SCHWEITZER: What about the problem of sameness, where it isn't as horrifying anymore because it is familiar?

LUMLEY: The job of the professional is to ensure that however familiar it is, still that one climactic scene gives you that original *frisson*. If he can do that, then he has succeeded. But if you finish reading the story and say, "Well, yeah. I've read that seventy-three times before," then it's a failure. There's bound to be many failures when you're looking for that one unique flash, that little bit of shudder down the spine. But there are bound to be, also, one or two genuinely good ones.

SCHWEITZER: Thanks for talking with me.

LUMLEY: You're very welcome, Darrell.

A SELECT SECONDARY BIBLIOGRAPHY ON BRIAN LUMLEY

Blackmore, Leigh. *Brian Lumley: A New Bibliography*. Penrith, N.S.W., Australia: Dark Press Publication, 1984.

Gosden, Simon. "Brian Lumley: A Bibliography of the Cthulhu Tales," in *Out of the Woodwork* no. 1 (1986): 14-15.

Jones, Stephen. "*Weird Tales* Talks with Brian Lumley," in *Weird Tales* 51 (Winter, 1989): 15-18.

Menzik, Clay. "Brian Lumley: A New Star in the Horror Galaxy: Interview," in *2AM* 5 (Fall 1991): 53-54.

Menzik, Clay. "Brian Lumley: An Interview," in *Eldritch Tales* 7 (1990): 19-21.

Price, Robert M. "Brian Lumley—Reanimator," in *Crypt of Cthulhu* 3:3 (Candlemas 1984). Reprinted: *The Horror of It All*, edited by Robert M. Price. Mercer Island, WA: Starmont House, 1990, p. 138-148.

Schweitzer, Darrell. "Brian Lumley: Disciple of Cthulhu," in *Fantasy Review* 10 (June 1987): 15-16.

VIII.

WILLIAM F. NOLAN

A WILLIAM F. NOLAN CHRONOLOGY

1928   William Francis Nolan born March 6, at Kansas City, Missouri.

1938   Begins writing stories about magicians, G-men, air aces, cowboys, etc. in school notebooks.

1942-45 Contributes to high school paper: poems, articles, and artwork. Wins all-city art award with his high school comic strip, "Freshman Frankie."

1945   Greeting card writer/cartoonist for Hall Brothers, Kansas City.

1946   Attends Kansas City Art Institute.

1947   Moves to California. Attends San Diego State College (now San Diego State University).

1948   Wins college art award.

1949-50 Commercial artist, mural painter in San Diego.

1950-51 Aircraft inspector for Convair, San Diego. Begins lifelong friendship with Ray Bradbury.

1952   Edits, illustrates, and publishes *The Ray Bradbury Review* (one-shot magazine tribute to Bradbury) from San Diego.

1953   Moves to Los Angeles. Attends Los Angeles City College. Begins close friendships with Charles Beaumont and Richard Matheson.

1953-54 Credit assistant, Blake Moffit and Towne Paper Co., Los Angeles.

1954   First published story, "The Joy of Living," in *If: Worlds of SF* (August). Freelance writer/artist for Whitman Publishing (Walt Disney comics line).

1955   Interviewer, California State Department of Employment. Begins selling fiction and nonfiction to men's magazines.

1956   With sale to *Playboy*, abandons art career to become a freelance writer in April.

1957   Wins trophy racing his British Austin-Healey in sports car event at Hour Glass Circuit. "The Small World of Lewis Stillman" printed in *Fantastic Universe*, which becomes his most widely anthologized story.

1958   First hardcover book, an anthology edited with Beaumont, *Omnibus of Speed* is published by Putnam's. Eventually writes eight books and more than 150 short pieces on sports/Grand Prix Racing.

1959   Enters television writing, with script sales to *The Twilight Zone* and *One Step Beyond*.

1960   Receives American Library Association citation.

1962   Uncredited co-editor with Beaumont on *The Fiend in You*, published by Ballantine.

1963   Science fiction collection, *Impact 20*, with Introduction by Bradbury, published by Paperback Library. Appears in *Year's Best SF*. Managing editor of *Gamma* (SF/fantasy magazine).

1964-70 Freelance reviewer for *The Los Angeles Times*. Selected for inclusion in *Who's Who in the West*.

1965   Two SF anthologies published: *Man Against Tomorrow* (Avon) and *The Pseudo People: Androids in Science Fiction* (Sherbourne Press).

1967   First novel, *Logan's Run* (with George Clayton Johnson), published by Dial Press. First major horror story, "The Party," appears in *Playboy* (April).

1968   SF anthology *Three to the Highest Power* published by Avon. MGM pays $100,000 for film rights to *Logan's Run*, which includes a Nolan/Johnson screenplay.

1969   SF anthology *A Wilderness of Stars* published by Sherbourne Press.

1970   Marries Marilyn Elizabeth Seal (now legally Cameron Nolan). Two SF anthologies published: *A Sea of Space* (Bantam) and *The Future is Now* (Sherbourne Press). Wins Edgar Award from The Mystery Writers of America.

1971   First SAM SPACE novel (SF/mystery), *Space for Hire* (Lancer) wins another Edgar Award. Edits SF anthology *The Human Equation* and Chad Oliver collection, *The Edge of Forever*, both published by Sherbourne Press. Returns to TV with script *The Joy of Living* for *Norman Corwin Presents*. Numerous TV and film credits follow throughout the 1970s.

1974   SF collection *Alien Horizons* published by Pocket Books. Scripts two-part miniseries *The Turn of the Screw*, filmed in London for ABC.

1975   Compiles/writes *The Ray Bradbury Companion* published by Gale Research Co. Honorary Doctorate from American River College, Sacramento, California. Scripts *Trilogy of Terror* for ABC, which wins Golden Medallion at the Fourth International Festival of SF and Fantasy in Paris, France.

1976 *Logan's Run* released by MGM; Bantam issues tie-in paperback (sixteen printings during the next two years). Writes screenplay (with Dan Curtis) for *Burnt Offerings*.

1977 SF collection *Wonderworlds* published by Gollancz in England. Sequel solo novel *Logan's World* published by Bantam. Wins Golden Scroll Awards from the Academy of SF & Fantasy for *Logan's Run* (Best SF Film of 1976) and *Burnt Offerings* (Best Horror Film of 1976). Wins Maltese Falcon Award for Dashiell Hammett biography. Scripts pilot show for *Logan's Run* TV series for CBS.

1978 *Burnt Offerings* wins Golden Medallion at the Tenth Annual Festival of Fantasy, in Spain.

1979 Selected for inclusion in *Who's Who in America*.

1980 Third solo sequel novel, *Logan's Search*, published by Bantam. Edits SF anthology (with Martin H. Greenberg), *Science Fiction Origins*, which is published by Fawcett-Popular Library.

1984 Horror/crime collection *Things Beyond Midnight* published by Scream/Press.

1985 Second novel in series *Look Out for Space* published by International Polygonics. Scripts *Terror at London Bridge* for NBC. "The Party" adapted for UNICEF Halloween Radio Show.

1986 Compiles *The Work of Charles Beaumont: An Annotated Bibliography & Guide* for The Borgo Press. Verse collection *Dark Encounters* published by Dream House. *Logan: A Trilogy* published by Maclay (omnibus, collecting *Logan's Run*, *Logan's World*, and *Logan's Search*); is also illustrated by Nolan.

1988 Special "William F. Nolan issue" of *The Horror Show* appears (Summer).

1989 Does audio reading of *Logan's Run* for Dove Books on Tape.

1990 Edits horror anthology (with Martin H. Greenberg), *Urban Horrors*, which is published by Dark Harvest. *How to Write Horror Fiction* published by Writer's Digest Books. Malibu Graphics begins LOGAN comic book series with adaptations of *Logan's Run* and *Logan's World*.

1991 Edits SF/fantasy anthology (with Martin H. Greenberg) *The Bradbury Chronicles*, published by Roc. Horror novel *Helltracks* published by Avon. Writes/illustrates chapbook *Blood Sky* for Deadline Publications. Special "William F. Nolan issue" of *Weird Tales* (no. #302, Fall) published. "The Party" cited by *Newsweek* as one of the seven most effective horror tales of the twentieth century.

1992　Third book in SAM SPACE series, *3 for Space*, is published by Gryphon. *Helle on Wheels* (chapbook) published by Maclay.

1993　Two hundredth anthology appearance (in *After the Darkness*). Official career commendation by Los Angeles Mayor Tom Bradley for "outstanding achievements in literature." Scripts NBC miniseries *The Black Summer* (from Peter Straub's novel, *Floating Dragon*). Scripts *Devil's Night* for ABC (from Clive Barker's "The Inhuman Condition"). Comic book *William F. Nolan's Beyond Midnight* published by Malibu Graphics.

1994　Horror collection, *Night Shapes*, published by CD Publications. Omnibus collection, *The Name Is Space*, appears from Maclay. Warner Bros. film *Yankee Champion* (adapted by David Cronenberg from a Nolan book) released. *Trilogy of Terror—The Movie* screenplay written by Nolan and Curtis. Mystery novel, *The Black Mask Murders*, published by St. Martin's Press, and is Nolan's 60th book.

A WILLIAM F. NOLAN INTERVIEW

SCHWEITZER: You mentioned in the introduction to one of your books that the essential characteristic for a writer of horror fiction is a love of the genre. So, how did your particular love affair with the field begin?

NOLAN: Part of that is already answered in "Dark Bedfellows," the memoir I've written for *Weird Tales*, how I fell in love with horror fiction by discovering Boris Karloff's *Tales of Terror* when I was a boy in Kansas City. But before that it was motion pictures. It was *Dracula* and *Frankenstein* in the early '30s. Those pictures had a tremendous effect on me as a child. The raising of the monster into the lightning in *Frankenstein* is imprinted in my brain, as is Harker's welcome to Dracula's castle and the whole effect and the mood of that sequence. I realized that horror was something I really related to emotionally. I would have to say that motion pictures started it all.

SCHWEITZER: When you became a professional, you gravitated toward screenwriting very quickly. So the fascination with film must have stayed with you all along.

NOLAN: Absolutely! When the MGM lion roared I used to sit in the Isis Theater in Kansas City and watch those early pictures thinking that someday my name would be up there on that screen. The first time I sat in the Cinerama dome in Hollywood and watched *Logan's Run* and the MGM lion roared and I saw "based on a novel by," and suddenly my name was there in giant letters—that was a great moment. I've loved films all my life. I still see two a week even now. Films are part of my life's blood. We live in a visual world, and as I wrote *Logan* I was envisioning it as a film. I write with an imaginary screen running inside my head, and each scene I write is a scene in my film with me playing all the parts, the director, the production designer, the actors, and so on.

SCHWEITZER: Your prose style is very spare. Is this intentional?

NOLAN: I never tell more than I need to in a story. I never over-describe anything. In the novella "Broxa" in *Weird Tales*, I give minimum description to each scene, so that the reader is told just what he or she has to know, and then the imagination takes over from there. I always leave room for the reader's imagination in my writing.

I literally do not understand the kind of British writer who opens the door to an apartment and spends the next five pages describing what's in the room, or writers who take half a chapter to get their character across a kitchen in a breakfast scene. I'm in and out of the kitchen and down the road and into the next county by the time they're reaching the marmalade. I can't write in that manner. I pare my work down to the essentials. I keep revising it until every word has a weight of its own. I try for very spare, economical images. The idea is to let the reader's mind create the rest of the image, so the reader thinks he or she is seeing more than I've actually written.

SCHWEITZER: What you're describing is the effect of film on prose. Compare this to a writer prior to the film era, say, Arthur Machen, who was gorgeous but very, very leisurely. He could take up half the story for the prologue.

NOLAN: I think that in terms of Machen and Charles Dickens and Algernon Blackwood and other early writers, or even Lovecraft to some extent, they were fine for their period. Readers were ready to accept that leisurely pace. When I wrote my first private-eye novel I had my detective moving through Los Angeles like a whirlwind, killing any number of enemies with his smoking .45 and having a great time doing it.

SCHWEITZER: Your new novella, "Broxa," has a considerable mixture of detective and supernatural elements. What do you see as the affinity between these two forms?

NOLAN: I'm a great cross-genre mixer. When I wrote the two novels about my Mars-based private eye, Sam Space, I cross-mixed genres—obviously science fiction and the hardboiled detective story. I love to take a form and put a new face on it to make it fresh. In "Broxa," I took the detective form and mixed it with the supernatural genre. I was able to do a semi-hardboiled detective approach within a demonic setting. It's a cross-mix, and I think it's fresher and allows the reader to find new trails to explore, new areas that he or she wouldn't expect to find in this kind of a story. Just about the time the reader thinks he's got one of my stories figured out, I always like to throw a twist into it, to knock him off his pins, as it were.

SCHWEITZER: I suppose the affinities are that the detective story is full of dark images and menace, only in the usual detective story it turns out to be a natural menace. So the affinity has been there from the start. Hence all the psychic detective stories.

NOLAN: That's true, but I think I've taken a new route with this novella. I've never read anything quite like it. I tried deliberately to freshen the whole genre of the private eye and the cliché of the missing-daughter case. The most overworked story in private-eye fiction is when the detective is hired to find a missing daughter. So I used that situation and turned it around. There are things in this novella that I'm sure no reader is going to guess. My wife said to me when

I was writing my second private detective novel set in Los Angeles, *The White Cad Crossup*, "You're two-thirds of the way through the book, so who's the killer?" And I said, "I don't know yet." She was shocked. "How can you write two-thirds of a novel and not know who the killer is?" For me, it works. I get right down to the last chapter or so, and then I look at all the different characters and I pick out the one the reader would least expect to be the killer. Then I tailor earlier portions of the novel to fit. It works.

SCHWEITZER: I take it, then, that you're one of those writers who sits down and gets going, rather than outlining.

NOLAN: It depends on the project. I outlined "Broxa" on about twenty-five file cards. What I often do is set up a basic plot skeleton. Then I flesh it out with the writing. I don't want a long, detailed outline, because that spoils the fun for me. I want to discover what is going on, along with the reader. Part of the fun is discovering what my characters are going to do next, letting them take me places that I didn't know they were going to take me. You decide to kill off a character, then you fall in love with the character, and end up letting him live. Vice versa, you think you're going to like a character, you don't like the character, so you kill him off. There's a god-like feeling to writing. You *are* God. You can create life or destroy it on the page. It's a tremendous feeling of emotional power.

SCHWEITZER: I think the secret, particularly in horror fiction, is to engage the emotions. A horror story that can't do that is nothing. So, how do *you* do that?

NOLAN: The first thing the writer has to do with any story is create real people. If you can draw your reader into the story by the reader's believing in your characters, if you can touch psychic nerves with people, touch fundamental truths with characterization, then you can do anything you want with those characters. The reader will go with you.

My first job as a writer, whether I'm doing short stories, novels, or scripts, is to find a way to create believable characters. If I can't do that, the reader's not going to care what happens in my story.

I had one letter, in which someone said they'd read one of my short stories in which I used five very short vignettes, and this reader asked, "How do you create such empathy so quickly for your characters?" Well, it's shorthand writing again. You have to make every word count. If you can create empathy in a paragraph rather than a chapter, then do it that way. Some writers require an immense amount of space in order to achieve in-depth characterization, but I do it very quickly. I sketch it in like a watercolorist. I suppose it's my art background. You know, I'm an ex-artist, and I think in visual brushstrokes. That's one way to put it: my style is a series of quick brushstrokes that build the picture stroke by stroke.

SCHWEITZER: Were you a professional artist *before* you became a writer?

NOLAN: Well, my first real piece of creative work involved both art *and* writing—for my high school newspaper. Called "Freshman Frankie," it was a comic strip that ran for twelve issues, and it dealt with this little fellow who wanted to be tall, and when he got to be tall nobody really loved him, so he went back to being small again. In other words, *be yourself. Don't try to be something you're not.* That was the message.

It won first prize in a city-wide high school contest back in Kansas City. This encouraged me to go on to the Kansas City Art Institute, where I studied art for two years. I became an artist for Hallmark Cards for a summer, designing and writing greeting cards. Then when I came out to San Diego in the late '40s, I set up my own art studio in Balboa Park. I painted outdoor murals and did commissioned artwork for various people. So I thought that was what I was going to be, a commercial artist. However, writing was the thing that I always enjoyed doing the most, but it was always in the background. Then in 1952 I realized that it was the *art* that should be in the background. So I reversed the entire course of my life. That's the day I admitted to myself that I really wanted to write for a living, not draw. My drawing now is purely on a hobby level. The writing is the career.

SCHWEITZER: Did you start sending stories out at that point?

NOLAN: Yes, the first story I sent out was in 1952. I have a very unusual sales record with regard to my fiction. I've written a hundred and fifteen short stories and I've sold a hundred and fifteen short stories! I've met people who have drawers full of rejected stories, but this kind of thing never happened to me. Sometimes an editor will say, "I know you don't have time to write a new story right now, so just give me one of your trunk stories, something you haven't been able to sell." And I say, "I don't have anything," and I mean it. I've written nine novels and I've sold nine novels. I don't understand how people can write ten, twelve, fifteen novels, and still have the guts to keep going when they haven't been able to sell them. It would have destroyed me. I haven't had that problem. I've sold ninety-nine percent of everything I've written in my life, fiction or nonfiction.

SCHWEITZER: You got into screenwriting relatively early, and so when you wrote *Logan's Run* you already had much more polish and discipline than the usual first novelist does. You already knew how to write by then.

NOLAN: Oh, sure. I learned by writing fiction first. I wrote in school notebooks from the age of ten. I wrote stories about cowboys and daring air aces and G-men. When I was ten and eleven I would fill notebooks with these lurid stories. They're dreadful things. I go back and read them and they show no jot of talent. But I just kept at it, learning more each year. I made my first sale when I was twenty-five and I had been writing fifteen years—all through high school and into college. But during this time I never sent out anything. When I felt that I was ready to send things out, then I began to sell immediately.

SCHWEITZER: Beyond horror and science fiction, you've written in several other fields, right?

NOLAN: Right. Most people don't realize that I've written eight auto racing books, and over a hundred and fifty auto racing articles. I've written in the show business field—biographies of John Huston the film director and Steve McQueen the actor. I've written westerns. I've written in the field of aviation, and of course I've done a lot of mystery writing, hardboiled detective, crime-suspense work, a biography of Dashiell Hammett, essays on Raymond Chandler and so forth. The answer is to do a lot of writing before you start sending out material, so you know you've polished your craft.

SCHWEITZER: At the same time, isn't there also a temptation to use this as an excuse for never sending *anything* out? Surely you've known writers like that, whose work is good, but they don't believe it and you have to pry it out of them.

NOLAN: That's certainly true of a lot of people. They simply won't work to get the material out. You've got to polish it. I start out with a Flair pen on paper at a coffee shop counter late at night. I do all my first drafts that way. I'm talking about novels, biographies, scripts, stories, whatever it is. I do them all with a Flair pen on a pad, handwritten. That forms one draft. Then I correct that handwritten draft, and I do another draft on the typewriter. I correct the typewritten draft, going over it very carefully, making yet another draft. I give it to my wife who has a word processor. I then correct her draft from the word processor, make a lot of changes, and then put it through the word processor once again. That's the draft that goes out to market. I don't see any other way to do it.

You've got to maintain a quality level. The writer I want to beat is William F. Nolan. I'm not too worried about Stephen King and Peter Straub and all these people. I'm worried about William F. Nolan. I've got to keep doing better than this guy, or else I'm not going to make it. I challenge myself each time out. Have I done this before? Is this fresh? Can I better the effect of this scene? Can I write a deeper character? Can I write a more shocking bit of dialogue here?

You've got to keep stretching yourself. The little voice inside you has to say, "You know you can do better. Now sit down there and *do* better." I know a fellow who has been writing for fifteen years, and he's done two short stories and part of a novel. That's it, and yet he calls himself a writer. But he isn't. He won't work hard enough. He just won't send out the material.

SCHWEITZER: I was thinking of someone on the order of Emily Dickinson. She never did send most of her material out, and it was all published posthumously. I suppose this can still happen, and sometimes dilettantes write interesting work. So you have to strike a balance between being over-confident and not confident enough. Perhaps a writer needs a genuinely effective way of evaluating his own work. How do you tell when your work is genuinely good? How do you know it's not just ego?

NOLAN: Let's talk about ego for a moment. Ego is absolutely the central foundation, the pillar that every writer has to have in his house. He's got to have that pillar of ego. He's got to believe he's good. He's got to believe that other people want to read what he has to say. It takes a lot of nerve to sit down and write something and expect that millions of people will want to read it or want to see it on the screen. You've got to believe in yourself. You have to believe that you have a vision, a fresh story to tell and a fresh way to tell it.

Ego is absolutely central to the continuance of a professional career. I have ego. I believe in myself. If I didn't, I don't think I could turn the work out.

In terms of how I judge it, I put on my editor's coat. I have a coat, the writer's coat, that I take off, and then I put on my editor's coat, and then I look at the story as if I'd never written it at all, as if someone else had sent it to me.

I've edited twenty-three anthologies and was managing editor of *Gamma* magazine in the '60s, and I've been contributing editor and West Coast editor to half a dozen other magazines.

As an editor, I look at this William F. Nolan story and say, "This guy is weak here. He's getting away with sloppy characterization there. He should tighten this sentence. Where's his motivation here?" I am able to be objective about my own work. A lot of writers aren't able to do that. When I put the editor's coat on, I catch a lot of things that the writer thought he could get away with.

SCHWEITZER: What was the story behind the magazine *Gamma*? This was an extremely interesting periodical which had only five issues, seemingly published with great stealth.

NOLAN: *Gamma* was a West Coast magazine created by Charles E. Fritch, who was to become a long-time editor of *Mike Shayne's Mystery Magazine* in later years. At the time he had never edited anything. This was in 1963. He got together with another writer named Jack Matcha, and myself, and the three of us launched *Gamma*. We put out five issues over a two-and-a-half-year period. It was supposed to be a quarterly. But we couldn't get the right distributor. Half the time the magazine never reached the newsstands of the country. These terrible distribution problems finally killed the magazine. But we had a tremendous group of writers: Fritz Leiber and Charles Beaumont and Ray Bradbury and all kinds of top people writing for it. The five issues that *do* exist are all of very high quality. I remember we had Shakespeare on one cover and William Faulkner on another. These are not names you usually find in such magazines.

SCHWEITZER: It was as if you were doing again what *The Magazine of Fantasy & Science Fiction* did in 1949, which was produce a science fiction and fantasy publication which was more literate than anything else on the market, and something you didn't have to make any excuses for.

NOLAN: You're on the mark! We used *The Magazine of Fantasy & Science Fiction* as our model. I read the first four or five years of that magazine cover-to-cover. It was like a bible to me. Our publication was a kind of West Coast version.

SCHWEITZER: How much of an influence was Ray Bradbury on your work? Did he ever coach you in the art of writing? One gets this impression from some of his introductions to your work.

NOLAN: Well, Ray was a great influence on me, as he has been on many people. Of course, I was influenced by a large number of writers, as most of us are. When you ask a writer the question, "Who influenced you?" he'll go down the list. I could do the same thing. I collect over a hundred authors in my own personal library. Bradbury definitely impacted my life at an early age. The first Bradbury story I read was "The Jar" in *Weird Tales*, and I thought that it was an extraordinary piece of work. I said, "Who is this man?" I began to read anything that had his name on it.

When I came out to California in 1950 and met Ray, he had just published *The Martian Chronicles*. I met him in July of 1950 and *The Martian Chronicles* had come out in May. He was just beginning his career, as it were.

But already I had read *Dark Carnival*, and many of his short stories in the pulps, and I told him I wanted to be a professional writer.

He said, "Well, look, when you have a story that you think is good enough, really good enough for a professional magazine to print, you send me that story and I'll give you a detailed critique." Well, it was three years later, when he went to Ireland, that I sent him "The Joy of Living" in an early draft.

He wrote back, "This is a fine story. Don't worry about being a writer. You're already a writer. You've gone through the early stages. You've learned dialogue. You've learned description. But what you haven't learned to do is end your story properly. You have the character doing X, Y, and Z, when he should be doing A, B, and C." He showed me, in a letter from Ireland, exactly how to end this story. And I took his letter and rewrote the ending; and the story became my first professional sale. It was printed in *If, Worlds of Science Fiction*, in 1954.

So Ray has had a great influence in my life. We've had many a long midnight conversation tossing ideas back and forth with Charles Beaumont and with Richard Matheson and with other mutual friends down the years. We formed a sort of West Coast writers' group that has included, from time to time, Ray Russell, Chad Oliver from Texas when he was getting his degree at UCLA, George Clayton Johnson, Ray, myself, Matheson, and Beaumont. We would all meet and stay up into the dawn talking stories, shouting and yelling out our ideas. I got a tremendous amount of help and moral support from those sessions. I look back on them with great fondness.

SCHWEITZER: For all horror seems to have been your first love, your first sale was science fiction. So what brought you to write SF at that time, as opposed to the *Weird Tales* kind of story?

NOLAN: There really was no market for it until Stephen King came along. He really created the modern market for horror. But horror, at the time I was writing in the '50s, didn't have the market that science fiction had, and a professional writer has to go with his market. You have to make a living at it. So I wrote a lot of science fiction, including *Logan's Run* and the SAM SPACE books, in that period. Now I am writing virtually no science fiction. I am doing almost entirely horror work, which is a return to my first love. I'm back home again now, and I'm going to stay there.

SCHWEITZER: Granting the fact that you *like* writing horror, what would you do if you found editors doing what they did to Frank Herbert late in life, that is demanding the same and more of the same, over and over?

NOLAN: I've never had any problems in that regard. I've had over fifty books published now, and I have several more in the works. Each is different. I don't repeat myself. John Steinbeck taught me that you can do all sorts of books and still maintain the same quality level, without having to repeat the same book over and over. I couldn't write a series of horror novels and nothing else. I will continue to write horror, but I will always write other types of material along with it. I'll always extend my roots out into other genres, because it's just natural for me. Otherwise I'd bore myself and I think I'd bore the reader.

I've written well over a thousand pieces of material, something like seven or eight hundred articles and the fifty books and forty television and film scripts, plus all the short stories. I've spread it out over many genres, but that's what keeps me fresh. That's what keeps the challenge alive in me, when I can switch genres, when I can get excited about a brand new thing.

SCHWEITZER: What are some of the things that you've done recently or will write shortly.

NOLAN: Let's start with David Kincaid, the protagonist of the novella "Broxa" *Weird Tales*. I'm going to write a series of novels about him and his involvement in various paranormal and supernatural adventures. In the last few years I've edited an anthology celebrating Bradbury's fiftieth year, *The Bradbury Chronicles*. *Blood Sky* was issued by Deadline Productions, with eleven pages of my artwork in it. My first horror novel, *Helltracks*, was published by Avon, and a collection of my best shock-terror stories, *Night Shapes*, was sold to CD Publications. I'm always doing new short stories: I've sold stories to about twenty anthologies. I'll had my own horror comic book, *William F. Nolan's Beyond Midnight*, published, and of course I continue to work in television, on *Movies of the Week*. Then there's verse, magazine articles, and checklists. I write every day. I write Christmas. I write New Year's. I write Halloween. The key to being a professional and the key to making a success out of this business is to write all the time. I expect to go on doing it for at least another twenty years. Then I just might start to slow down!

SCHWEITZER: Thank you, William F. Nolan.

A SELECT SECONDARY BIBLIOGRAPHY ON WILLIAM F. NOLAN

Clarke, Boden & James Hopkins. *The Work of William F. Nolan: An Annotated Bibliography & Guide.* San Bernardino, CA: The Borgo Press, 1986.

Clarke, Boden & James Hopkins. *The Work of William F. Nolan: An Annotated Bibliography & Guide, Second Edition, Revised and Expanded.* San Bernardino, CA: The Borgo Press, 1995.

Elliot, Jeffrey M. "Interview: William F. Nolan," in *Fantasy Newsletter* 4 (February 1981): 10-13.

Elliot, Jeffrey M. "Nolan's Run," in *Night Voyages* 1 (Winter/Spring 1983): 46-48.

Elliot, Jeffrey M. "Nolan's Run: Interview," in *Questar* 3 (June 1981): 62-64, 73-74.

Gorman, Ed. "Interview: William F. Nolan, Joe R. Lansdale," in *Mystery Scene Reader no. 1.* Cedar Rapids, IA: Fedora, 1987, p. 130-135.

Houston, David. "Interview with the Logan Man: William F. Nolan," in *Future* 4 (August 1978): 20-25.

McSherry, Frank D. "William F. Nolan," in *Twentieth-Century American Science-Fiction Writers*, edited by David Cowart. Detroit: Gale Research Co., 1981, Vol. 2, p. 48-53.

Nakamura, Joyce, ed. *Contemporary Authors Autobiography Series, Volume 16.* Detroit, MI: Gale Research Co., 1992. Contains Nolan bibliography following his autobiographical life/career essay.

Nolan, William F. "Afterthoughts on *Logan's Run*," in *Science Fiction Review* 6 (August 1977): 32-33.

Nolan, William F. "Dark Bedfellows: The Horrors of My Life," in *Weird Tales* 53 (Fall 1991): 9-11.

Wiater, Stanley. "William F. Nolan," in *Dark Visions: Conversations with the Masters of the Horror Film*. New York: Avon, 1992, p. 119-128.

Yenter, Charles E. *William F. Nolan: A Checklist*. Tacoma, WA: Charles E. Yenter, 1974.

IX.

MANLY WADE WELLMAN

A MANLY WADE WELLMAN CHRONOLOGY

1903   Manly Wade Wellman born May 21st of missionary parents in Kamundongo, Angola.

1927   Begins career as reporter and reviewer for various Kansas newspapers, *Wichita Beacon, Eagle*, etc.

1927   First published fiction, "Back to the Beast," in *Weird Tales* (November).

1930   Marries Frances Obrist, June 14th.

1931   "When the Planets Clashed," Wellman's first science fiction story, published in *Wonder Stories Quarterly* (Spring).

1934   Becomes full-time, freelance writer, which he remains for the rest of his life.

1936-38 Assistant project supervisor, WPA Writers Project, New York.

1937   Only son, (Manly) Wade Wellman (Jr.), who also became a writer, born.

1940   *Twice in Time* published in *Startling Stories* (May); later published in book form by Avalon, 1957.

1943   "The Devil Is Not Mocked" published in *Unknown* (June); later dramatized on television.

1944   "The Golden Goblins," first JOHN THUNSTONE story, published in *Weird Tales* (January).

1946   *Romance in Black* (as by GANS T. FIELD), his first book, published by Utopian Publications, London, a reprint of the 1938 *Weird Tales* serialization, also bylined GANS T. FIELD. Wins Ellery Queen Award for *Star of a Warrior*.

1950   *The Beasts From Beyond* published by World Distributors, England, a reprint of *Strangers on the Heights*, from *Startling Stories* (Summer 1944).

1951   *The Devil's Planet* published by World Distributors, reprinted from *Startling Stories* (January 1942). "O Ugly Bird!," the first JOHN THE BALLADEER story, published in *The Magazine of Fantasy & Science Fiction* (December).

1956 Wins Edgar Award for Best Nonfiction Study of Crime for *Dead and Gone* (1955).

1962-69 Instructor of Creative Writing, Elon College.

1963 *Who Fears The Devil?* published by Arkham House.

1964-71 Instructor of Creative Writing, University of North Carolina.

1973 *Worse Things Waiting*, a major retrospective collection of supernatural fiction from the pulps, published by Carcosa. Wellman wins the Award of Merit from the American Association of Local Historians for *The Kingdom of Madison*.

1975 *Worse Things Waiting* wins the World Fantasy Award for Best Collection. *Sherlock Holmes's War of the Worlds* (a collaboration with his son, Wade Wellman) published by Warner.

1977 *The Beyonders* published by Warner.

1978 Special "Manly Wade Wellman issue" of *Whispers* (no. 11/12; October) published.

1979 *The Old Gods Waken* published by Doubleday (first JOHN THE BALLADEER novel, dubbed "Silver John" by Doubleday publicists, to Wellman's disapproval).

1980 Wins World Fantasy Award for Lifetime Achievement. *After Dark* published by Doubleday (another JOHN THE BALLADEER story).

1981 *Lonely Vigils*, a collection of Wellman's pulp series character stories (JOHN THUNSTONE, JUDGE PURSUIVANT, etc.) published by Carcosa. *The Lost and the Lurking* published by Doubleday.

1982 *The Hanging Stones* published by Doubleday (a JOHN THE BALLADEER story).

1983 *What Dreams May Come* published by Doubleday (first JOHN THUNSTONE novel, reviving series from 1940s pulps).

1984 *The Voice from the Mountain* published by Doubleday (a JOHN THE BALLADEER story).

1985 *The School of Darkness* published by Doubleday (a JOHN THUNSTONE story).

1986 Wellman dies on April 5th. *Cahena*, his last novel, published posthumously by Doubleday.

1987 "Where Did She Wander?," the final JOHN THE BALLADEER story, published in the anthology *Whispers VI*, edited by Stuart Schiff. *Valley So Low: Southern Mountain Stories* is compiled by Karl Edward Wagner and published by Doubleday.

A MANLY WADE WELLMAN INTERVIEW

SCHWEITZER: Did you ever want to be anything else before you became a writer, or were you set on it from the start?

WELLMAN: Well, there were times when I was little that I wanted to be a cowboy, a deep-sea diver, and things like that, but I think I always wanted to write ever since I could string a few letters together into words. I think I was trying to write stories when I was six years old.

SCHWEITZER: How long before you were serious about selling them?

WELLMAN: It's hard to answer that because I wrote all through school, between the things anyone did, like studying, or in my case, playing a lot of football. I wanted to write, and I had observed the fact that there were magazines and people were being published in them and paid for it. When I was in college—that was a long time ago, during the Calvin Coolidge administration—I sold my first stories.

SCHWEITZER: What attracted you to writing supernatural fiction?

WELLMAN: I think I've got to go way back to my beginnings. I was born in Angola. My parents were medical missionaries. The people—who, by the way, were wonderful people—were full of wonderful stories of men who changed into leopards, a skull up in a tree predicting the future, and so on. I would listen to these things and it took hold of me, and I never lost it. When I came back to this country when I was a little boy, I lived out in rural places and I always had an ear for such material, and I've stayed with it ever since. I hope I still have an ear for it. I love to hear something new in the way of folklore, legendry, and so forth.

SCHWEITZER: Did you begin immediately with American folklore? This is what you're best known for now.

WELLMAN: Yes, I did. After all, despite the fact I was born over there, I am an American. My heritage is Southern American. I was writing about what I ran into and what I heard. Yes, if I have a reputation at all, it is as a Southern regional writer. I have written a few stories about Africa, but even though the memories are vivid, I was a little boy and it was long, long ago. God knows things are different in Angola now.

SCHWEITZER: Is the tradition you are drawing on still alive and growing, or are people just preserving the stories?

WELLMAN: I think we're getting farther and farther away from it all the time. We don't realize the fact that we're getting away from folklore. The places are getting settled up. The old days in which there was a fixed habitat are going away. You know what I mean—you'd be born there and live, and die there. You'd grow up and in the little town or little country community you'd meet a girl and marry her and have children, and when you died, you'd leave the farm to your son. The people to whom I listen—I go up into the North Carolina mountains—are older people. The young ones are sophisticated. I think there had better be a stronger and more intelligent effort than there is now to preserve our folklore because it's going away. Everybody is going to be like everyone else sooner or later, watching the same television programs, wearing the same clothes, even speaking with the same accents, I suppose. I hate to see regionalism go, but why deny that it is going?

SCHWEITZER: Do you think the new society will develop its own folklore?

WELLMAN: We're developing it all along. Look at the jokes you hear about computers. We have, of course, lived up to and made legends reality. For instance, flying to the moon. I can remember when I wrote stories about a flight to the moon and these were considered extravagant. It is now commonplace. A flight to Mars will be commonplace. But as to the supernatural, it has already become quaint. I have known people in my youth who have believed in witches and werewolves. Now, I don't know many who do actually believe these things, although they're interested. They're curious about them. It becomes another way of life, and I suppose more folklore will develop. I think folklore exists in big cities, and some very interesting folklore, although I'm not a city man and don't write that.

SCHWEITZER: How do you think belief in the supernatural effects the writing of it? There's one school of thought which says believers can't write it because they take it for granted, and cites Aleister Crowley's novels as an example. Then there are those who say you must at least half believe or you won't take it seriously at all.

WELLMAN: About that, Montague Summers said you have to believe in ghosts to write about them. He added in a preface to one of his books that he had seen a ghost. I go along with M. R. James, a writer I very much admire, who said he would be willing to consider the evidence if it was presented to him. By which I gather that he had no particular belief. Nor do I know what to believe, but I'll go along with M. R. James. If someone wants to show me that there is such a thing as a vampire or a werewolf or a ghost—I've never seen a ghost, although once or twice I thought I was pretty close; I've done my best to see them and gone to haunted houses and so forth—I'll consider it. I'm a skeptic, but I'm not closed-minded about it, nor do I think anyone should be.

SCHWEITZER: You had a novel in *Startling* in 1944 called "Strangers in the Heights," and there was something in the author's column about strange things happening while the story was being written. What about that?

WELLMAN: It happened in South America, as you'll remember, and there is always something interesting and grotesque coming up from South America. There were little pieces in the paper at that time about what seemed to be werewolves in the mountains of South America. You know how you can take a little germ of something like that and light a shuck and take off with it. When it comes to that, may I say that most of my stories have at least some kind of a basis in what somebody thinks is fact.

SCHWEITZER: How much did Farnsworth Wright [the editor of *Weird Tales* during its "golden age," 1924-40] influence what you wrote and how you wrote it?

WELLMAN: Farnsworth Wright was a great joy. He was the best editor I ever had, and I think I can say that because I had a great many editors and very fine ones. Wright bought from me when I was in college. He was a man who would make up his mind if you were worth fooling with. Now, I was pretty raw, but he worked with me. He made me revise and he would go into little minor nuances of a story and perhaps ask you to bring something up. He was very critical, but he was constructively critical. On top of that, he was a tremendously erudite man and he would know what he was talking about in this field, and as close as you can be friends with an editor, he and I were friends. I considered him a fine gentleman and I remember how deeply I mourned him when he died.

SCHWEITZER: What do you most remember about him?

WELLMAN: Wright was a tall, gaunt man and he had, I believe Parkinson's Disease. Anyway he shook all the time. He was never still. His whole body trembled. The point is you would soon forget this because he was a man of great charm. He was quiet; he was strange; but he was *sui generis*. There has never been anyone like that. In fantasy publishing today, editors pay little attention to the kind of man Wright was and the things he did.

SCHWEITZER: Editors today still do ask for revisions and try to develop people. How did Wright differ in this?

WELLMAN: Well, if he wanted a story from you, he would stay with you to the bitter end. My wife Frances wrote a story for him, and he sent it back repeatedly. There was one character, an old priest, and he wanted her to bring him out and make him vivid. He got three revisions from her, which means four drafts, and then bought it and sent her a check and sent the story back and said, "Revise it again." Frances sat down and did. The story, which was published in England in 1980, called "Don't Open That Door," in fact underwent another revision for the British editor. Let's use the word "painstaking." I won't say that he was soft on anybody. Now, there were people from whom he didn't ask much revision. Augie Derleth used to say he would send it and Wright would buy it. I think he bought pretty much whatever Lovecraft sent him, and he should have. Without Lovecraft it wouldn't have been *Weird Tales*. Frank Belknap Long worked with him. Most of the people I know paid attention to what Wright said and he didn't scruple to say it, and if he worked with you he sure-to-God didn't baby you. And if a story wasn't for him, he wouldn't fool with it, but he might say as he said to me one time, "Get back and write me something else." What I'm saying is that a lot of editors are like this, but a lot of them are not. If they look at it and don't want it, they'll pop it right back to you and start looking at something someone else has written. I think the point about Wright was that he was doing a very special kind of magazine and he was shooting the works. He was dedicated. And there never was a magazine like *Weird Tales*, and I'll say again, Wright was the best, the most rewarding editor I ever had.

SCHWEITZER: How did you get along with John Campbell?

WELLMAN: Campbell, of course, was a very good editor, but I didn't terribly like him. What John liked to do was pitch you a curve. He'd give you an idea for a story and have you go and write that. He wasn't so enthusiastic for what you thought of yourself. I think he had a very good mind for these, although if that's what's going to happen, you're going to have a lot of idea stories. I never had any squabbles with John. Some of the things he believed in, I didn't, and don't to this day. Politically and socially, there were different things, but he was a very splendid and very successful editor. On top of all that he was an oddball.

SCHWEITZER: What made you turn to science fiction?

WELLMAN: I was writing that mostly because I wanted to. It appealed to me, and I was reading H. G. Wells, Jules Verne, people like that, when I was a boy. I don't know. Looking at you, why are you interested in this sort of thing? One just gets that way. I remember a lot of people thinking this was odd in me and asking, "Why are you writing about these things which could never possibly happen?" The only point is they've all possibly happened. We *have* flown across space. We *have* split the atom. We *have* done wonderful things and terrible things, we human beings, and these things which are commonplace today were all imaginatively predicted long ago. Well, I wrote it because I wanted to write it.

SCHWEITZER: What is the primary appeal of the supernatural story for you?

WELLMAN: The sense of wonder, and of course, the sense of terror. There aren't very many supernatural stories that aren't frightening. On the other hand, some of them are kindly little stories, but look here: you watch a Walt Disney picture—I mean back yonder when Walt was still at it doing something like *Snow White*. The most impressive things were the frightening things. You read *Alice in Wonderland*. You think what a delightful little dream story it is, but you do notice all the terrible things that are just hanging at the edge of perception, like the moamraths. You'll hear one of them cry out if you go down in the woods, and if you hear it once you'll be quite content. Or the crow that shut out the sky flying over Tweedledum and Tweedledee and how they ran. There is terror in these things. There is terror in the little stories we tell our children. Jack climbing the beanstalk—had the giant found him he'd have eaten him. I wonder what that goes back to? What in the beginnings of this race? A fear of cannibals? These things are all there, and, by the way, kids love it. They love scary things and eat 'em up.

SCHWEITZER: Did you have any conscious literary influences when you started writing, or did you just write the sort of stories you heard orally?

WELLMAN: Of course I've written a lot of other things besides fantasy and science fiction, but I think early on the things that influenced me were Rudyard

Kipling, Jack London, Arthur Conan Doyle—these representative things that you would read—and as I said, H. G. Wells. I ran into him pretty early. As I got along and became mature, well, I go along with what William Faulkner said, that you'd better read James Joyce's *Ulysses* the way a Baptist preacher reads the Bible. The books I read, or rather re-read, are by Hemingway, Thomas Wolfe, William Faulkner, and some of the English writers. I'll say that the novel that made the biggest impression on me—I was about eighteen when I read it—was *The Long Journey* by Johannes V. Jensen, which, by the way, is full of the supernatural and is in itself a sort of story of Mankind.

SCHWEITZER: A movie was made of *Who Fears the Devil?* I have not seen it, but I haven't heard much good about it. What did you think of it?

WELLMAN: Congratulations on not seeing it! I didn't have any quarrel with the movie people. They were nice fellows, but looking at it I think it's one of the ten worst movies I've ever seen. I think they missed the point a lot. I remember that at about the same time that I saw it (the movie was called *The Legend of Hillbilly John*)—they came and had a preview in my home town of Chapel Hill—I saw a movie called *Fiddler on the Roof*. Now, I'm not Jewish, but I can appreciate these things, and I saw that here was a wonderful capturing of the folkways of a little Jewish settlement in pre-World War I Russia. And I thought to myself, "Why can't we do the same thing for an American folk theme instead of messing it all up with a bunch of trained seals in Hollywood?" No, it wasn't a good picture, and I don't know anybody who thinks it really was. They wrote in a lot of things themselves that just aren't true about the mountain people.

SCHWEITZER: Did it suffer from Hollywood stereotyping and caricaturing? That's precisely what I would expect would have happened to it.

WELLMAN: That's precisely what it suffered from.

SCHWEITZER: The Beverly Hillbillies Syndrome?

WELLMAN: As a matter of fact, I think that was where they got their idea of what mountain people are like. Okay, I greatly respect the mountain people. I love them. They're a virile, proud, self-respecting people. They can be pretty rough. If you want to get hurt, you can go about it in the right way up in the mountains and get yourself killed, but they are a tremendously individual bunch of people. Their way of life is being modified and passed away. I can't think offhand of a good movie I ever saw about the Southern mountain people.

SCHWEITZER: Are these characteristics you describe the reason why so much folklore has been preserved among them when the rest of the country has lost it?

WELLMAN: It's been preserved because people haven't gotten back in. The little corner of the Southern mountains where I go whenever I get a chance is not developed. For instance, there aren't any factories there. There's no tourism. When I went up there before, some of my friends helped me build a cabin there—I had no place to stay unless I was going to stay at the house of a friend, and I did—and am very grateful for that. It was provincial and very insular, but it has flavor. I don't know whether it's all going to be swallowed up in the next few years or not. I only wish it wouldn't, but what good does it do you to wish?

SCHWEITZER: Presumably, then, you'll continue to write stories of their folklore as long as you can?

WELLMAN: At this meeting I heard that the third of a series of novels about John is going to be published by Doubleday, as soon as I get it written, and editors, when they come up to me, talk about this particular thing, this regional country stuff. Although I have seen some editors flatly say they didn't want any hillbilly stories. The word "hillbilly," by the way, up in the mountains, until very recently at least, was an insult. If you went up where I go and called a man a hillbilly, you got out of there the best way you could, because he thought it was his born duty to take the neck out of your body. However, we know what hillbilly means. So, I won't write for that editor.

SCHWEITZER: The term has always sounded condescending to me.

WELLMAN: Yeah, it's like sticking racist names on different ethnic groups. I've always refused to be called a hillbilly, and I've always refused to be called a cracker. Don't anybody try it, not even in my old age.

SCHWEITZER: What's a cracker?

WELLMAN: Well, that's a term for Southerners. I used to hear it in the army, and somebody called me a cracker in the army, and after that he never called me one again.

SCHWEITZER: What do you think about the current health of the fantasy field?

WELLMAN: You know how we sit around here and talk about how we don't have so many magazines, but a great many magazines in the mainstream will buy fantasy, and there seem to be some people around here making a living out of it. Now, it was very hard indeed back, let's say, in the 1930s. As a matter of fact, if you were a freelance writer then, you were apt to make everything grist for your mill and write other things than fantasy and science fiction. And I've done that. I've written historical novels, some very highly realistic regional novels, and a lot of Southern history, and some books for boys. The whole point is that a writer has to live, whether you see the necessity or not, and he has to think about money. When you hear writers at this meeting talking to their agents, talking to their editors, the talk is always money. After all, it's a capitalist world and we need it. But I think that fantasy does have a strong hold. The right kind of editor on a new magazine, I think, would do very well. If you had a Farnsworth Wright or a John Campbell. What you need is editorship and you need it in a very high degree.

SCHWEITZER: Do you feel that too many writers in the modern field are repeating the past?

WELLMAN: I know what you mean. You mean people are writing about the Cthulhu Mythos and writing pastiches of Robert E. Howard. I don't awfully like to see that done. It seems to me that new themes are badly needed. But what are the new themes? Somebody you always used to hear quoted claimed there were only thirty-eight basic plots and the Greeks used them all. I'd like to see a list of the thirty-eight basic plots, but I don't think that there's going to be any defense by readers or editors either against first-class writing. There never was, and I don't think there ever will be, and there is some very fine writing indeed being done in this genre today.

SCHWEITZER: What are your immediate plans?

WELLMAN: My immediate plans are to finish the third JOHN THE BALLADEER novel. Indeed, I must. After that, there are other projects, not all in fantasy. I don't know. I've got years of work ahead of me, and somehow I've got to get it done. I don't think there's any point in not having some kind of future. Do you?

SCHWEITZER: Thank you, Mr. Wellman.

A SELECT SECONDARY BIBLIOGRAPHY ON MANLY WADE WELLMAN

Benson, Gordon Jr. *Manly Wade Wellman, the Gentleman from Chapel Hill: A Memorial Working Bibliography*. Albuquerque, NM: Galactic Central, 1986.

Coulson, Robert. "The Recent Fantasies of Manly Wade Wellman," in *Discovering Modern Horror Fiction 1*, edited by Darrell Schweitzer. Mercer Island, WA: Starmont House, 1985, p. 92-105.

Elliot, Jeffrey M. "Manly Wade Wellman: Better Things Waiting," in *Fantasy Voices*. San Bernardino, CA: Borgo Press, 1982, p. 5-18.

Jones, Stephen. "Better Things Waiting: An Interview with Manly Wade Wellman," in *Fantasy Media* 2 (May/June 1980): 14-16.

"Manly Wade Wellman," in *Contemporary Literary Criticism, Volume 49*. Detroit: Gale Research Co., 1987, p. 386-398.

Meyers, W. E. "Manly Wade Wellman," in *Supernatural Fiction Writers*, edited by E. F. Bleiler. New York: Charles Scribner's Sons, 1985, p. 947-954.

Meyers, W. E. "The Silver John Stories," in *Survey of Modern Fantasy Literature*, edited by Frank N. Magill. Englewood Cliffs, NJ: Salem Press, 1983, Vol. 4, p. 1744-1748.

Phelps, Donald. "Interview: Manly Wade Wellman," in *Pulpsmith* 3 (Autumn 1983): 18-26.

Waggoner, Diana. "Got Tell It on the Mountain: The Achievement of Manly Wade Wellman," in *Fantasy Review* 9 (April 1986): 17-19, 50.

X.

CHET WILLIAMSON

A CHET WILLIAMSON CHRONOLOGY

1948 Chet Williamson born in Lancaster PA.

1966 Graduates from Elizabethtown Area High School.

1970 Graduates with B.A. degree in English from Indiana University of Pennsylvania. Marries Laurie McCandless (June).

1977 Begins employment with Armstrong World Industries (till 1985). Son, Colin McCandless Williamson born, Dec 20.

1981 First professional story sale, "Offices," published in *Twilight Zone* (October).

1985 Becomes full-time writer.

1986 *Soulstorm* published by Tor.

1987 *Ash Wednesday* published by Tor.

1988 *McKain's Dilemma* and *Lowland Rider* published by Tor.

1989 *Dreamthorp* published by Dark Harvest and Avon.

1990 *Reign* published by Dark Harvest. Special "Chet Williamson issue" of *Weird Tales* (no. 298; Fall) published. "Yore Skin's Jes Soft'n Purty...He Said" is nominated for the World Fantasy Award.

1994 *Ravenloft: Mordenhelm* published by TSR. *Second Chance* published by CD Publications.

A CHET WILLIAMSON INTERVIEW

SCHWEITZER: I seem to remember you from Lovecraft fandom in the middle '70s. You weren't writing modern horror fiction then, or at least I didn't know about any. So, what *were* you writing at the outset of your career?

WILLIAMSON: I was always a *real* big fan of Lovecraft's. I was in the Esoteric Order of Dagon, which is an amateur press association dedicated to Lovecraft and weird fiction. I belonged from about 1973 to 1983. I didn't really start to write fiction seriously until around 1979 or 1980, when I started writing short stories. My first sale was to *Twilight Zone* in 1981. That's what started it. I began my first novel in 1982. That was the real start.

SCHWEITZER: What novel was that?

WILLIAMSON: *Soulstorm.*

SCHWEITZER: You seem to have started writing much later in life than a lot of people do, presumably your mid-twenties at least. So, what did you plan to do with your life before you knew you were going to be a writer?

WILLIAMSON: I started out wanting to be an actor. I *was* one for many years; I was a member of Actors' Equity. I did a lot of summer stock and regional shows and industrial shows, and through doing the industrial shows I began to *write*. I was doing comedies, parodies—even a *sci-fi* one about people in business—to be performed at business conventions. And when I began to realize that I was constructing plots and characters, I thought, well, why not do this in real fiction? So I did, and it took me a while to get to the point where I was producing stuff day after day, but eventually I did and it got to the point where I enjoyed being a creator more than I enjoyed being an interpreter.

SCHWEITZER: When you started writing fiction for yourself, did you know from the start that you were going to be a horror writer, or did you try other things first?

WILLIAMSON: No, I didn't try other things. I've loved horror since I was a kid. The stock-boy in my grandfather's grocery store terrified me with Edgar Allan Poe stories in the basement. I discovered very quickly the Ballantine horror anthologies that were out in the early '60s. Lovecraft was being reprinted then. So with my love of horror and my interest in Lovecraft, it was only natural with my interest in Lovecraft that when I started to write, I would write horror. It just seemed to be the thing that appealed most to me.

SCHWEITZER: I can't help but wonder: did the stock-boy read you the stories or enact them?

WILLIAMSON: He *told* them. He was a very good storyteller, and the cellar itself was a really scary place because it went back to lower levels and got darker and darker as it went. As I got older I explored more, back into the deeper cellars. It was a great place to hear Poe.

SCHWEITZER: Since you got into all this by way of Lovecraftian fandom, it surprises me that you didn't turn out large numbers of Cthulhu Mythos stories narrated in the First Person Delirious by scholarly Rhode Island recluses who get eaten by Things at the end. Why not?

WILLIAMSON: When I think of influences, I have to say that Lovecraft really wasn't an influence in my writings. I think it's because I didn't start writing fiction until later in life. This is just my theory, but I think that when you're younger you tend to copy the kind of fiction you enjoy. I started relatively late, so I had already formed an outlook—I wouldn't call it a world-view—and I was also influenced by contemporary fiction as well. I had read a lot of horror, not just Lovecraft. It's funny, though. I was reading Peter Cannon's new book on Lovecraft, the TWAYNE AUTHORS SERIES volume, and I came to the discussion of *The Picture in the House*. Now, I hadn't read this story for years and years, and of course the climax concerns the blood dripping through the ceiling. And I remembered that, and I thought, "Gee, in *Dreamthorp*, I have a scene in which blood is dripping through the ceiling onto a velvet hat," and I wondered if that image might have been an influence. But *then* I remembered, "Wait a minute. I dreamed that." I had a dream, and had written it down, thinking that someday I might use it in a book. But, one step backwards: Was the dream inspired by my memory of Lovecraft? So I got a copy of *Dreamthorp* and a copy of *The Picture in the House*. *The Picture in the House* describes it as *a large, irregular patch that slowly dripped crimson* and in my book it was *a large, irregular spot from which the blood dripped*. So, phrases and images just lodge in your mind and they might pop up years later, because I'm sure that when I was a kid and read that story for the first time, it made a tremendous impression on me. I must be influenced more than I know...

SCHWEITZER: But you still didn't write about large tentacular seafood and add new books to the Mythos library of eldritch tomes.

WILLIAMSON: No. I saw that as a dead end. I had read so much of that kind of material, and after a while there's a real sameness about it. It wasn't the kind of *believable* horror that I wanted to write. Also, it's understood only by a very small group of readers. From the beginning, I wanted to get a wider readership than people who are only into the Cthulhu Mythos, the Yog-Sothoth Cycle of Myth.

SCHWEITZER: I think the limitation of that sort of stuff is that no one other than Lovecraft ever actually wrote a scary one. The artistic development of the Mythos ended in 1937.

WILLIAMSON: I think you're right. Most of them aren't very frightening. The worst wind up being silly in-jokes, and the best are literary exercises that are very well done, but fun for only a few readers.

SCHWEITZER: This gets back to something Les Daniels suggested, that no one becomes a horror writer simply because it's an expedient way to make money, or for any conscious, deliberate reason. We do it because we're *warped*. We're that way from the beginning... Obviously your fascination with the dark cellar and Poe when you were a kid meant you were one of us.

WILLIAMSON: Unfortunately, I had a very happy childhood... [*laughs*] But I was always fascinated by the dark side, and as soon as I could go to the movies alone, I saw all the American International matinee Poe films. I bought the early issues of *Famous Monsters of Filmland*. I built the Aurora models. I fell in love with all that kind of stuff. Yeah, I was warped. My parents, God love 'em, took me to see *Psycho* when I was eleven and it scared the *hell* out of me. I don't think they knew how scary it was going to be. It was great. And there was *Thriller*, which was on TV when I was fourteen. I ate that stuff up like crazy.

SCHWEITZER: You were fortunate in that your parents allowed you to be exposed to that sort of thing. I was very strictly *not* allowed, but turned out this way *anyway...* You may well be better adjusted in your warped nature.

WILLIAMSON: [*Laughs*] That may be. My parents were pretty permissive in what they let me read. But at that time you could feel pretty safe that if you bought a horror novel you were not going to find explicit sex and violence in it. It was more suggestive. I remember that when Monarch Books came out with their series of *Gorgo* and *Reptilicus* novelizations, there was *sex* in those. My mother always did keep a watch on what I read, and she went through *Reptilicus*, and when she came upon the *roseate nipples*—that was the last of *Reptilicus*. She let me keep the cover... That was around 1961, so they were spicy by the standards of the era. But today it's a little harder. Kids are so inundated with graphic horror—you've got eleven- and twelve-year-old kids who've seen all the *Friday the Thirteenth* and *Nightmare on Elm Street* movies, and the suggestive horror, which I really find more frightening, just doesn't affect them. Hopefully, with a little age and maturity, it might, but the explicit stuff seems to have a desensitizing effect on a lot of kids.

SCHWEITZER: I suppose what sums up the current state of the movie field for me was one of those instant-remainder coffee-table books that I saw in a store, about horror films with lots of photos and the like—the image on the cover (to instantly define to the browser what the book was about) wasn't a werewolf or the Frankenstein monster; it was a *knife* descending. So the public's whole idea of what horror is no longer has anything to do with the supernatural as much as it does with spurting arteries.

WILLIAMSON: Yes, you're right. The stuff that gives me the chills, the *frisson*, is the supernatural and the suggestion of the supernatural. Did you see *The Lady in White* a couple of years ago? It was wonderful, a pure supernatural film. There was a physical element of menace in it, but there was an awful lot of the supernatural in it. I hadn't seen that kind of movie in ten, twenty years. And it was *genuinely chilling*. To me, M. R. James is still able to produce the shivers. There are some stories I can read—and the climax is just the realization that you were talking with a dead person, with a ghost—but it's so skillfully done and so realistic that it really does produce a shiver. That's a subtlety that I'm afraid is lost in a lot of stuff today, in films primarily, but also in the literature. It's a shame.

SCHWEITZER: At least a high-quality, subtle horror novel is still commercial, in the way that a similar film probably isn't.

WILLIAMSON: Absolutely. I think there is room in the field for both kinds of work. I think you can have the most explicit, graphic horror and still have a fine book. You can also have very subtle, sophisticated suggestion and have it be just as good. It all depends on the writer and the way he or she approaches the material. I think the movies are skewing our view of it a little bit. They seem to be the primary vehicle for horror just now, rather than books.

SCHWEITZER: Yet for the first time we have a horror category in publishing, and multi-millionaire horror writers.

WILLIAMSON: There aren't that many of them, really. You can count the multi-millionaire horror writers on probably three fingers. Of course, Stephen King is the one who is always pointed to, but King is so absolutely unique in the way his career has gone and the magic he has cast on readers. It's a thing that hardly ever happens. He's the bestselling author of our time. But if you look at the bestseller list at any one time, you only find a few names associated with horror novels. The lists are loaded with techno-thrillers and romances, and the Danielle Steeles and Sidney Sheldons and James Micheners. So horror is making some inroads, certainly. If people are becoming aware of horror, and the horror bestsellers are leading people to seek out other such books, great, but I'm not all that convinced that's happening. I think you'll find people who read everything Stephen King writes, but won't necessarily go out and look for more horror novels. It's the same sort of person who reads everything Tom Clancy writes, but doesn't go out and search for other good techno-thrillers.

SCHWEITZER: Still, the big change has been that for the first time writers are making *careers* as horror writers, whereas even someone like Algernon Blackwood, who wrote lots of horror, also wrote children's books and other things completely out of the field. But now there are writers who are expected by their publishers to turn out a new horror novel every eighteen months or so, one right after another. I can't help but wonder how long any writer can keep it up.

WILLIAMSON: I don't know. I can only answer for myself. I write on spec, so I don't *have* to turn out something every so often. I see myself continuing to deal with the darker side of humanity, but whether I'll continue to write what you could classify as pure horror novels, I don't know. I think as you continue to write, you have to continue to grow and learn. Once you stop—and start, in essence, to write the same book over and over again—some of the best part of life has stopped.

SCHWEITZER: Horror is basically a single mood or note, and I wonder if anyone can make a career over, say, twenty years, striking the same note. *The Haunting of Hill House* seems to have just *happened* in the middle of Shirley Jackson's career. She could not have written twenty-five of them.

WILLIAMSON: No, of course not. I don't see on the other hand how someone can write twenty-five or thirty mysteries. If I had the kind of career Agatha Christie had, I'm sure I would have gotten really bored writing puzzle mysteries all my life.

SCHWEITZER: I have a theory, which may apply more to someone like John Creasey, who wrote many hundreds of mysteries, and that is that such a writer has only one trick. That's all he can do, and he doesn't feel the emotional textures of the story, and is really not a *storyteller* at all, but a puzzle-constructor. But the horror writer is very much exploring emotional experiences and textures which can't necessarily come on cue, let alone several hundred times.

WILLIAMSON: That's one of the reasons I like horror more than other genres. It seems that in other genres you're limited in some way. In a mystery you're limited to solving a problem. Whether you're writing hard-boiled or tea-cozy, there's a crime that has to be solved. In a western you're limited to a certain historical place and time. In science fiction, although the borders of that are a lot less strict than other genres, generally you're working in terms of the future. But horror is a literature of emotion, and emotions can take place anywhere at any time. You can have a horror western, horror science fiction. You could have a horror romance, of all things. It's a very wide-ranging genre. What you tend to *find* mostly is contemporary horror. The worst of it is indeed contemporary, one-note, the kind of books that are written over and over again. But that's a very narrow part of what horror can be. For that reason I don't mind being called a horror writer, because horror is just an emotion.

SCHWEITZER: For marketing purposes, it would seem that if you set a horror novel in, say, Minoan Crete, it wouldn't be published as a horror novel. It might be published as fantasy, or as a historical. This would determine what sort of cover it would get, where and how prominently it would be displayed in the publisher's catalogue, and even how big an advance you got for it. Or whether or not the publisher would accept it at all.

WILLIAMSON: You may be right. I'm dealing rather ideally in my definition of it, but still I think that I can go anywhere I want with it. Hopefully if you try to take a change in direction, readers will follow you. There are a lot of readers who want just a straight horror novel, though. So if someone who normally writes in a certain way does something very different, those readers are disappointed. They might not read the next book. But that's a chance you have to take.

SCHWEITZER: There's a theoretical point I've always wondered about, which is what would have happened if, well into his career, Stephen King wrote the equivalent of *The Sound of Music*. How would his enormous readership, brought together out of an interest in his horror novels, suddenly take a light, romantic comedy from him? Would he be able to sell it? What would his editors do? They'd be tearing their hair out.

WILLIAMSON: King took a change of direction with the *Gunslinger* series. That is not the typical contemporary horror that he's been doing, but the books are selling well and readers are following him. Admittedly it's not as radical a change as writing a light, romantic comedy, but I think if he did write a comedy, an awful lot of his readers would go along with him. I value that, because they've found an author who has a voice that they like. Like them, I tend to read *writers*. I don't read genres. If there's a writer whose work I like, I'll read whatever he's written, no matter what genre it's in, because I like his voice. I like the way he tells a story.

SCHWEITZER: Well, you've written in other genres. You even had a story in *The New Yorker*.

WILLIAMSON: Yeah. Humor. Al Sarrantonio just picked that up to reprint in *The Fireside Treasury of New Humor*. And I've written one suspense novel. I may do another; I may not. I've also written some science fiction, but my heart is really in the horror field. That's what I enjoy doing the most, what I feel the most comfortable with. As long as I have a passion for it, I'll continue to write it.

SCHWEITZER: Could you give our readers a quick run-down of some of your novels?

WILLIAMSON: Sure. *Soulstorm* was the first one. I had to work on a relatively small scale with that book, because I didn't want to get lost in a large cast of characters and many locations. So I thought the classic haunted-house story would be a good place to start. There are a lot of influences which I think can be seen in that book, more so than in my later ones. It's a real head-bashing horror kind of thing, not too subtle, but I think a lot of fun. My second novel, *Ash Wednesday*, was a more thoughtful book. What I wanted to do was a passive horror story, in which there are no monsters, no things that come after you. The situation is that one day a small town wakes up to discover that all its dead have returned as semi-transparent, naked wraiths. They don't move. They don't speak. The entire action of the book is dependent on the reactions of the people in the town to these intimations of mortality. The third book was *McKain's Dilemma*, a suspense novel set in Lancaster County where I live. That was an attempt to create a very realistic private eye. The fourth was *Lowland Rider*, which was a descent-into-Hell story; in this case Hell being the New York subway system, which I certainly look on as pretty hellish. Then there's *Dreamthorp*, which is a lot more graphic and explicit than anything I've done to date. It had to be, because I was dealing with a sociopathic killer. In that one, also, the protagonist turned out to be a woman. I hadn't intended that, but she took over the book, and I was very glad. The story is ultimately her triumph.

SCHWEITZER: There sure are a lot of novels about sociopathic killers of late. It seems to be a trend: *Koko* and *The Kill Riff* and most especially Rex Miller's *Slob* and *Slob II: The Revenge of Slob* or whatever it was, and so on. I assume that you wrote yours without any deliberate intent of copying any of these. It must be something in the air.

WILLIAMSON: Yeah. It is something in the air. Fiction reflects society, and this is so much in the news today. The book, I must emphasize, is not solely a sociopathic-killer book, although he does feature in it. It's a book mainly about people who are searching for a home, a haven, and the kind of love that one finds there, including the killer. Sociopathic killers need love too... But, yes, it's so much around us today that I suppose it was inevitable that one of these fellows would eventually creep into one of my books. I don't expect to write another one. But you have to do it once.

SCHWEITZER: Surely no writer can allow himself to follow trends. You have to either make trends or stand alone, and the rest is sheer luck.

WILLIAMSON: I think you're right. I try very hard not to be imitative. Originality is a very valuable commodity to me and to readers. I would like a reader to finish a book and not merely close it and go on to the next one, but to think about it a little because he or she hasn't read anything quite like that before. They say that there are no new plots, and it's true in a way, but there are and always will be good new ways of retelling the old ones.

SCHWEITZER: How does the technique of the horror novel differ from that of other types?

WILLIAMSON: A lot of people have said that they write horror primarily to scare the reader. I don't. That's one of the furthest things from my mind. If the reader wants to be scared and my books keep him awake at night, that's fine, because it shows that I've touched inside them. But primarily what I want to do is write a novel, and I don't especially care if it's a horror novel or not. But because of the way I think, that's what it's probably going to be. What I'm mainly concerned with are my characters, and their problems, and the way they solve them. Primarily I want to tell a good story with characters that are going to interest the reader from the beginning and make him or her stay with me till the end.

SCHWEITZER: Are there any more arbitrary techniques or requirements? I am thinking of the case of Raymond Chandler's *Playback*, which was making his publisher really frustrated because it was supposed to be a mystery and there wasn't even a corpse until halfway through. So, are there any things you have to do in that sense of pacing—at what point do you introduce a menace, and so on?

WILLIAMSON: If I can, I like to introduce a menace as early as possible, and then go back and fill in the pieces. There should be some sort of menace or hint of it—in a genre horror novel—on the first or second page. But also on the first or second page—and what is more important to me—there has to be a real person doing something which the reader becomes interested in. It is not totally necessary to have the menace on the first page. If you can just interest the reader enough to keep going, tell an interesting story, then the menace will come. Depending on the way it's packaged, they *know* that a menace is going to come, so, in a way, holding it off longer and longer may make it all the more frightening and powerful when it finally comes, because of the slow, gradual buildup. But it all depends. You can have a murder take place on the first page and go terribly explicit and have it work just as well. I don't think you should be limited by any particular framework.

SCHWEITZER: You're limited by the mere fact that this is a horror novel. In real life, if something strange starts happening, we do not immediately assume that vampires or Nameless Things are responsible, but in the horror novel, since the reader knows this *is* a horror novel—I mean, it's got one of those black, embossed covers and it says *horror* quite clearly on the spine—the reader is going to come to that conclusion quite quickly, perhaps well before the characters plausibly can. Therefore, if you don't follow up that conclusion fairly quickly, your characters are going to seem awfully dense. So the *pacing* of reader expectations may be a function of category.

WILLIAMSON: I see what you mean. But if the character jumps to the conclusion too quickly, the character looks like a New Age Shirley MacLaine-following bozo. You have to anchor it securely in the real world. In the real world, most sane, rational people are not willing to accept the fact of a vampire or a werewolf—neither of which I've used. You'd be willing to accept *anything* before that. You'd accept the most bizarre psychological explanation, the weirdest conspiracy theory, before you would admit to the existence of the supernatural.

So there has to come a point in the book where there is no other solution. It's like what Sherlock Holmes said about when all other explanations have been ruled out, whatever remains, however improbable, has to be the answer. So there has to be that moment, and hopefully with the pacing that moment will come before the reader finally tosses the book down and says "Boy, what a thick-skulled dimwit." So, yeah, there is some skill and craft involved in getting to that point.

SCHWEITZER: This is actually the classical Lovecraftian theory of horror, that the real horror isn't so much the big, menacing thing with claws, but the implications of what that thing's mere existence means to our view of reality.

WILLIAMSON: That's right, and in the books where I use supernatural menaces of any sort, I try to make the most shattering moments come at the realization of, "My God. This is real. This exists." It's just as hard for the reader to believe that—you do suspend your disbelief when you read a horror novel, to some extent—but to *really* make the reader suspend that disbelief, the writer must make the characters convincing and well-developed and have them in the same position as the reader would be in, in the same state of disbelief, to make it effective. When that moment comes, your whole view of life is completely turned around.

SCHWEITZER: Which would preclude the possibility of a New Age horror novel. Skepticism on the part of the writer and the reader seems to be required, or else both will take the supernatural elements completely for granted, and there won't be any build-up or suspense or shock.

WILLIAMSON: Sure. If all these things exist and we believe in spirits and entities under every bush, where does the interest arise? What's so wonderful, so awesome about an intrusion from the supernatural world?

SCHWEITZER: What would happen, then, if more and more of your readers start to actually believe in this stuff—if Shirley MacLaine wins?

WILLIAMSON: I like to think she won't... [*Laughs*] But whether you are a New Age believer or a rational human being, you can still enjoy a good novel in any genre. So I don't see that as much of a problem. I'd be happy to have New Agers read my books and take them for what they're worth—to them.

SCHWEITZER: Yet it would seem that horror fiction itself is the product of a culture which does not believe in the supernatural. Back when everybody did, there was no horror fiction, as in, say, medieval Europe. Fritz Leiber has a thesis that John Webster was the first horror writer. He was writing in the 1620s. There was then just enough skepticism that people could begin to play games with the supernatural, and use it to symbolize psychological states, and so on, although most people still believed in the Devil. Yet disbelief had crept in just enough. This may also explain why no one is writing horror fiction in, say, India or central Africa today—for all they are writing novels—because everyone still believes in the supernatural.

WILLIAMSON: I never really had thought of that. Reading horror requires some skepticism, because horror is about shaking people up and questioning their established beliefs, and the suggestions that there are more things in Heaven and Earth, Horatio. So of course in a world where everyone believed explicitly in ghosts and demons and witches, there would be no need for horror, because there would already be that cleansing that I think horror does to people's everyday lives.

SCHWEITZER: Ultimately what the rational people are afraid of more than anything else is the possibility that Shirley MacLaine is right.

WILLIAMSON: [*Laughs*] I see what you mean. But my books are all essentially about the fear of death, the fear of separation from someone you love, the fear of being ill or disfigured. Very realistic fears. It's not the fear of ghosts, but the fear of what the thought of ghosts represents. In a way ghosts are nice, because they insure life after death. But the vampires, the werewolves, the demons all represent death and destruction. *That* is the harsh reality, no matter what society we're in. I think we use horror as a kind of palette from which to paint those very real feelings. If you were to tell someone, "This is a novel about how we deal with the inevitability of death," I think they would put that sucker down and go find the next Garfield book. But if you can couch it in a horror novel or in a story supposedly about the supernatural, they'll find it much more accessible and easier to swallow, but what you're saying will still come through.

SCHWEITZER: What are you writing just now?

WILLIAMSON: I just finished a novel dealing with professional theater, which I was involved with for a number of years. It is a horror story, although it tends to verge more into the mainstream. The next novel, which I am planning now, you may not even call a horror novel. It has elements of horror in it, but it also has a touch of fantasy, a touch of thriller. Hopefully the scope is a bit larger than some of the things I've done before. I think it might have an appeal to a wider audience. I hope.

SCHWEITZER: Thank you, Chet Williamson.

A SELECT SECONDARY BIBLIOGRAPHY ON CHET WILLIAMSON

Bromley, Robin. "Breaking in: Chet Williamson," in *Twilight Zone* 6 (August 1986): 56-57.
McDonald, T. Liam. "Profiles in Terror: Show Me the Dead Men: Chet Williamson's Rising Star," in *Cemetary Dance* 2 (Summer 1990): 30-38.
Wiater, Stanley. "Chet Williamson," in *Dark Dreamers: Conversations with the Masters of Horror*. New York: Avon, 1990, p. 201-208.

XI.

F. PAUL WILSON

AN F. PAUL WILSON CHRONOLOGY

1946   Francis Paul Wilson born in Jersey City, New Jersey, May 17.

1969   Marries Mary Murphy.

1971   First professional fiction sale (horror), "The Cleaning Machine," in *Startling Mystery Stories* no. 18 (March). First science fiction sale, "Higher Centers," in *Analog* (April). First comic script in *Eerie* no. 34 (August).

1974   Begins practicing as a physician in Bricktown New Jersey.

1976   First science fiction novel, *Healer*, published by Doubleday.

1978   *Wheels Within Wheels* published by Doubleday.

1980   Wins Prometheus (Libertarian) Award for Science Fiction for novel *Healer*. *Enemy of the State* published by Doubleday.

1981   *The Keep* (first horror novel) published by Morrow (August).

1983   Unsuccessful film version of *The Keep* released. Directed by Michael Mann.

1984   *The Tomb* published by Whispers Press and Berkley. Makes *The New York Times* bestseller list. Short story, "Soft," published in J. N. Williamson's anthology *Masques* marks Wilson's return to the horror short fiction field.

1985   *The Tomb* wins Porgie Award from *The West Coast Review of Books* as best paperback original novel.

1986   *The Touch* published by Putnam (June). Novella, "Dydeetown Girl," published in *Far Frontiers IV* (January).

1987   "Dat-Tay-Vao" published in *Amazing Stories* (March). "Traps" published in *Night Cry* (Summer). "Dydeetown Girl" is a Nebula Award finalist.

1988   "Dat-Tay-Vao" and "Traps" are both Bram Stoker Award finalists. *Black Wind* published by Tor (September); Stoker Award finalist in 1989. Three new Wilson novelettes featured in the *Night Visions VI*.

1989 "Glim-Glim" (original teleplay) aired on *Monsters* (January 30). *Black Wind* is a Bram Stoker Award finalist. Novel version of *Dydeetown Girl* published by Easton Press and Baen Books. *The Tery* (novel version) published by Baen.

1990 *Reborn* published by Dark Harvest and New American Library. "The Barrens" published in *Lovecraft's Legacy* edited by Robert Weinberg. *Midnight Mass* published by Axolotl Press. Wilson volume of AUTHOR'S CHOICE MONTHLY #13, *Ad Statum Perspicuum*, published by Pulphouse. "Pelts" published as a chapbook by Footsteps Press.

1991 *Reborn* and *Sibs* published by Dark Harvest. "The November Game" in *The Bradbury Chronicles*, edited by William F. Nolan. Original Wilson stories appear in *The Ultimate Frankenstein*, *Dark At Heart*, *Masques IV*, and *Borderlands 2*. *Reprisal* published by Dark Harvest.

1992 *Nightworld* published by Dark Harvest. *The LaNague Chronicles* published by Baen Books. Special "F. Paul Wilson issue" of *Weird Tales* (Winter 1992/93) devoted to him. *Freak Show* (anthology) published by Pocket Books. *The Barrens* published by Wildside Press.

1993 *Sister Night* (retitled from *Sibs*) published by NEL (UK).

1994 *The Select* published by Morrow.

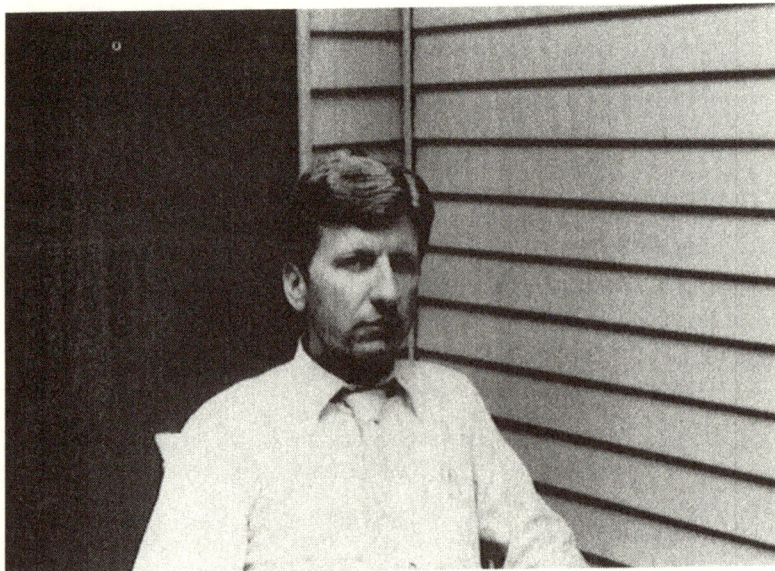

AN F. PAUL WILSON INTERVIEW

SCHWEITZER: Tell me about your recent books.

WILSON: The most recent book is *Sibs*. Before that there was *Reprisal*, then *Reborn*. Probably as this issue of *Weird Tales* is coming out there will be *Nightworld*, which ties up the dark fantasy or horror universe I've been working in. I've linked up six books into a single cycle. It's taken eleven years to write. I'm amazed that I could do it. I didn't intend them to be linked together when I started out.

SCHWEITZER: *Black Wind*, published in 1988 left many readers wondering whether you're following the trend in the horror field away from supernaturalism into straight thrillers and crime/psychological fiction.

WILSON: No. *Black Wind* was just the next book that was ready to be done at that time, and frankly it didn't do that well. Tor certainly got enough copies out into the stores, but an awful lot of them came back. The timing was bad because it was sort of a pro-Japanese novel and there is growing anti-Japanese sentiment in the country. But, while I still would like to stay with supernatural fiction, I don't want to repeat myself. That becomes a problem, trying to avoid doing the same book over and over again, or slightly different clones of the same book. I don't know. At this point, I have taken much of the summer and fall off and am taking stock. I'd like to write a variety of things, but I'm not sure the publishers will cooperate.

SCHWEITZER: You'll notice that most of the great supernatural writers of the past—Machen or E. F. Benson or Blackwood—didn't have *careers* as supernatural writers the way publishers want writers to now. They didn't just turn out one horror novel and then another and another throughout the whole of their writing lives. A contemporary horror novelist, beginning in his late twenties, might well be expected to write forty or fifty horror novels by the time he's seventy-five. I'm not sure that's possible.

WILSON: I agree. I suppose you can just keep on writing the same book over and over again. Certainly we know science fiction authors who have done that and gotten away with it, but, unfortunately, I haven't had a plan in my career so far. I think it shows. Some publishers have even told me that I don't write the same stuff often enough. In other words I may stop and I may write a science fiction novel, and then I may do something like *Sibs*, which is much more street-level and has a very small weird element to it. Or I should say it has a very large weird element, but a very small hint of the supernatural. You're not sure if there's anything supernatural going on or not. I've talked to a few publishers, or batted a few ideas off a few publishers recently, and anything that doesn't sound like what I've done before is met with coolness.

I think that all of us who have had any sort of sales record have run up against that. You are expected to do more of what sold well for you in the past.

SCHWEITZER: I should think that sooner or later you will become unable to do what you did before, and will end up writing increasingly ineffective pastiches of your former work. Possibly some mystery writers, Agatha Christie or John Creasey, for example, could write the same books forever, but since horror is a matter of mood and emotion rather than an intellectual construct, once the sincere feeling is dulled through repetition, the books won't scare anybody anymore.

WILSON: True. You lose the freshness. I just finished Ed McBain's *Tricks*, which is his umpteenth 87TH PRECINCT novel, all of which have the same formula. All these multiple storylines weaving in and out another until finally everything comes to a conclusion. He can do those *ad infinitum*, and they still remain interesting. But in a horror novel, with that single focus and emotional intensity that you have to maintain, it can wear you out. You find that even with the most visceral material, you can become repetitive in your descriptions. You have to be careful about that. Horror is a much more wearing type of fiction than, say, science fiction, which I've written, too. Horror can exhaust you. I could see going on and on doing more SF much more easily than the intense supernatural horror I've been working with.

SCHWEITZER: Perhaps the reason for this is that what is currently marketable as horror is very narrow in its focus. You know, ordinary people in a contemporary American frame of reference, as opposed to, say, a horror novel set in twelfth-century Greece. I gather that non-contemporary settings are a bit of a taboo in this business.

WILSON: I imagine that it is, although I've gotten away with a lot. *The Keep* is set in Eastern Europe during World War II. *The Tomb* shuttled back and forth between the Raj in India, the Sepoy Rebellion of that time, and modern-day Manhattan. So I've been able to mix genres and toy with history. *Black Wind*, which is borderland horror but is really a historical novel, started in 1926 and went up through World War II. I have gotten to stretch in that sense, but, again, they want me to do more historical horror novels. The problem is that my interests are in certain periods, and once I've tapped them out, I don't necessarily want to go back to them.

SCHWEITZER: You're a victim of your own success then.

WILSON: That's very true. When you run up against an instance where the sales figures of the new book aren't as good as for the previous one, you can feel the publishers turning on you. I've gotten to see now that in this current climate the publishers tend to look at your past sales figures and *then* read the book. If those figures aren't what they want to see, it really doesn't matter what this current book is. They decide not to buy it. I'm not a consistent bestseller by any stretch, but I do have a sizeable core audience for my horror. Even with that goofy cover, *Reborn* managed to sell a couple of hundred thousand copies. But I know other writers whose sales have slacked off, and they've seen doors slammed in their faces. They are good writers and are still doing good work. But past performance seems to count more than what you're submitting.

SCHWEITZER: Does the writer then end up at another house with a smaller advance, or does he become unable to publish at this point?

WILSON: In this market, he's becoming unable to publish. There are already plenty of other writers at the other house with the smaller advance. Your timing has to be right. You have to be there firstest with the mostest. I think this is temporary. I think it will turn around, but a lot of editors are looking over their corporate shoulders. They're feeling the chill wind of the Recession and no one is going to stick his or her neck out.

SCHWEITZER: This suggests that a new writer might be better off under some circumstances with less money. If you get a $500,000 advance for your first book, then all your subsequent books must sell well enough to meet such a figure. But if you started off at $20,000, chances are you can always meet expectations.

WILSON: That's very true. In a sense, you feel very sorry for the writer who gets a large amount on his first novel, because he has to live up to that, right away. The publisher will demand something similar and just as strong. You are much better with a smaller starting advance, internally and externally. Externally so you can build on those smaller successes, and internally it can mess up your head to get that kind of initial success without really having earned it or felt you have paid your dues. Getting a lot of rejections on the way up toughens you. When you finally do make a score, you feel you've earned it. But no matter what kind of dues you've paid, a huge advance can screw you up personally. That kind of windfall can have the devastating effect of solving all the day-to-day problems that were distracting you from what's really wrong with your life.

SCHWEITZER: Let's imagine that right now Stephen King suddenly writes a fluffy, romantic comedy, something as innocent as *Mary Poppins*. Assume it's very good, a masterpiece of its type. What would King's publishers *do*? Wouldn't they be on a spot?

WILSON: Well, they would publish it and put a nice pricetag on it, and it might go the way of *My Pretty Pony*, which I have just seen selling for half-price.

SCHWEITZER: I'm not sure that's a good example, because the regular edition of *My Pretty Pony* was badly-produced, poorly-illustrated, over-priced, and "limited" to something like twenty-five thousand copies. At fifty dollars a copy, it wouldn't move. At fifteen dollars, it might have.

WILSON: Maybe there's a limit to what people will buy because King's name is on it. But when you're talking about King, you're talking about a pop-cultural phenomenon. He seems to exist apart from the market pressures that affect us mortals. If you'd said Dean Koontz or Peter Straub, you'd get a totally different answer, because while they do sell in very high figures and Koontz reaches number one on the bestseller lists, neither of these writers is an icon like King. But if the book was good, I think King could carry it off.

SCHWEITZER: Surely when the writer is actually writing the book, he can't afford to think too much about these sorts of marketing considerations, or he'll go nuts.

WILSON: You have to be true to your story. But no one writes in a vacuum, so you can't ignore your market. Those are the realities. If you write to be read, and obviously if you are sending your work out to a publisher you intend to be read, you have to give some thought to the people who are going to read you. If you have an established readership in a certain genre, I think you have to take them into account.

When I switched from science fiction and did *The Keep*, I didn't have to worry about that. I was leaving behind my entire readership and going into new territory where I would be selling to people who had never heard of me. It was a nice, free feeling that I was not carrying a karmic burden from my writing past. I think that whenever you write in a genre you do carry a certain burden from other writers, the ones who shaped that genre, but I had no baggage of my own to bring along, and the publishers had no baggage that they brought to the manuscript in what they expected. Now, whatever I do, somebody's expecting another *Keep*, or looking for it and hoping for it.

SCHWEITZER: It seems to me that you have two advantages, the first being that if things got really bad in horror, you could go back to science fiction where you would be welcomed with open arms; and the other is that you're probably not economically dependent on writing since you're also a full-time physician.

WILSON: True. If I never sold another book, my mortgage would still be paid. My children's education is assured. But writing becomes a part of your identity after a while. Whether it's an economic necessity for me or not, it's also a part of who I am and what I do and how I spend a good part of my life. Having that taken away, not so much given up but taken away in the sense that I could no longer sell and no one wanted to buy my books, would be equally as crushing as if it were a financial catastrophe.

SCHWEITZER: At what point in your life did you start writing? Was it before or after you became a doctor?

WILSON: I actually started writing around age six or seven, in the first grade. I wrote little stories then. My first story was a haunted house story. I wrote stories off and on through high school. In college, I was pre-med when I decided I really wanted to sell something. The idea then was to sell one story. Then I would be a published author and I could get on with my medical career.

It took me years, and I finally sold a story to John W. Campbell at *Analog* in 1970, and by that time, after all those years of trying, I became hooked. So I was actually a published author before I was a doctor. I was in medical school then. I didn't get my degree for a few more years. During my internship I didn't get a chance to write a word. You're working twelve hours a day, twelve days a week—no, I should say you work twelve days in a row, then get two days off. There was no time for writing then, but once I got into group practise some time did free up and I did *Healer*. From then on, I've been balancing the two careers, making time, and just trying to enjoy both and do both well.

SCHWEITZER: Has your medical career influenced your writing career other than by competing for time?

WILSON: Being in family practice, I am in contact with people on an intimate basis four or five days a week, and it's a wide variety of people. So my contact with the human species and its variations is pretty broad and, as I said, pretty intimate. It helps with an ongoing appreciation of people. I certainly do pick and choose little pieces of them for characters. I'm not a terribly social person, so if I was a full-time writer, I might see very few people on a day-to-day basis. So it helps keep the humanity in my work.

SCHWEITZER: It also gives you convincing details. Your story "Soft," for instance, shows a lot sound medical speculation.

WILSON: Not always so sound. I showed it to Shawna McCarthy and she picked up on an anatomical error right away. I had this person turn into a blob of flesh lying on a bed, and he was still breathing. Shawna said, "His ribs are gone. How could he breathe?" I thought about it for a second, and I said to myself, "Damn it. She's right." So, I went back and put in a few ribs and bones left to hang his diaphragm on so it could still have something to pull against. But, to use another example, in *The Keep*, Dr. Cuza suffers from scleroderma. I've seen scleroderma patients. I know how it affects their personality, what it does to them. It also gave me a lot of good little bits to do with this character. In that sense, certainly, that extra knowledge, that dimension of how human physiology works certainly helps. But I'm not interested in writing medical thrillers and I'm not interested in writing about doctors, *per se*. I did it once in *The Touch*, and that was fun, but otherwise my writing is my golf game. It gets me away from my practice. I don't really want to write about diseases.

SCHWEITZER: You are writing more about the region you live in, though. I can't think of too many people writing horror about the New Jersey Pine Barrens.

WILSON: Robert Dunbar has a book out called *The Pines*. That took place in the Barrens. But I've used the setting in a number of stories, in "Pelts," in "The Barrens," and I also used it in the *Freak Show*, which ends up in the Pine Barrens. But it's a fascinating place with an enormous amount of history, and truly Lovecraftian in the sense that you have enclaves of people who have probably not seen civilization, and who do inbreed. It's much more overstated in some of the stories about the place than really happens, but there really are, definitely, people you can look at and say, "Well, somebody's brother and sister got together on that one."

SCHWEITZER: I'd think that with that sort of inbreeding, the result would just be an exaggeration of whatever was running in the family, longer noses or whatever.

WILSON: It's probably overstated, but there are some really strange-looking characters out there in the Pines. And they're truly living off the land in every aspect. They eat what what grows wild and they kill what runs wild. Their contact with civilization is coming out to get kerosine or gasoline and buying some clothes and boots. Then they high-tail it back into the barrens.

SCHWEITZER: Can they be that isolated in a state as small as New Jersey? Surely they watch the same TV, shop in the same malls, etc. as the rest of the population.

WILSON: No. No electricity. They have kerosine stoves. They wouldn't have TVs without the electricity. Some of the more sophisticated ones may have a generator and perhaps a battery-operated radio, but we're talking about one to two million acres of virgin land just off the Northeast corridor. There are places, they say, where a human eye has yet to see, out in the barrens. It's that unexplored. There's nothing in there and only hunters go in there anymore. The people who originally settled the barrens were outcasts; they were chased in there.

SCHWEITZER: How much personal exploration of the area have you done and how much contact have you had with people like the ones depicted in your story, "The Barrens?" Are these your neighbors and patients, or are they people you have to seek out?

WILSON: I've seen some of them, and I've done some driving through the Barrens, but a lot of stories, like the Pine Lights, I've picked up from descriptions. I know hunters who swear they have been out there in the night and have seen the lights going through the sky, going from treetop to treetop. And I know hunters who have run into the people out there, and they say they're pretty scary, in the sense that they're very suspicious. They seem quite hostile and they do not welcome company out there. What was that Lovecraft family...?

SCHWEITZER: The Whateleys?

WILSON: The Whateleys.

SCHWEITZER: The degenerate side of the Whateley family.

WILSON: I could see the Whateleys out there and even some people from Innsmouth, coming up the Bass River from the ocean. I haven't actually spoken to any of the wild Pineys. Now there are Pineys who are definitely civilized, but they still live in the Pines. The ones who live in the small towns, they have electricity, they watch TV; they're somewhat homogenized like the rest of us, but they've got nephews or distant relatives in the backwoods and the off-roads that they don't necessarily speak about, but they know they're back there, and they're living their own lives.

SCHWEITZER: What sort of supernatural legendry comes out of this region, other than the Pine Lights and, of course, the Jersey Devil?

WILSON: I went into some of it in "The Barrens." Virtually any of the stories I told were true, in the sense that I didn't make them up: the Witch of the Pines and things like that. Mostly I take stories that are available and give them a little twist, or take off from them and use them as a springboard. But the lore of the pines is not so much supernatural as has to do with robbers and thieves and Tories and some of the old Lenape Indians.

SCHWEITZER: Could you get as much material out of this as Manly Wade Wellman did out of the southern Appalachians?

WILSON: I don't think so. I guess there is a richer culture in the Appalachians. The pine culture isn't as extensive. They have their applejack and they have their stories of the Jersey Devil and stuff, but a lot of them are isolated and there isn't that deep a vein to mine, at least not to my mind.

SCHWEITZER: Do you travel around while researching novels? Did you, for instance, go to Romania for *The Keep*?

WILSON: No. For *Black Wind* I did. I went to San Francisco and I bit the bullet and went to Hawaii and researched Honolulu and Pearl Harbor and places like that. Most of my research in *The Keep* was gleaned from people who had been to Romania or who used to live there, and from books. I used some of the techniques I'd learned in science fiction to make it realistic and give it a patina of reality. I guess I succeeded. When the movie company was looking for locations, they called me and asked where was the Dinu Pass, which was a fictional location near the Transylvanian Alps where I had set the story. The book had convinced them there was such a place.

SCHWEITZER: The movie version of *The Keep* was not notably successful. Any comments on why?

WILSON: I've been over this a lot and I get crazy whenever I start talking about it; but Michael Mann, who seems to have a great visual sense, had no sense at all of this type of story and how to tell it. He doesn't seem to have much sense of how a story is constructed. He just wanted to do what he wanted to do, and he did not want any mention of a vampire in the movie. Even though a vampire is just a red herring in the book, he wanted no mention of it at all. So if you do that, you take away the very reason that the book is set in the Transylvania Alps, which is to highlight this red herring. As a result, things start to crumble. He did not build character. He did not tell a coherent story. When I read the script, I wrote to him and I pointed out all of this to him in a very gentle, non-ego-trampling way, I thought. But he ignored me, and when I did make a visit to the set, he was very cool. I don't know if he felt threatened, or what, but he wanted no input at all from anyone. It was to be a Michael Mann picture. As a matter of fact, in some of the pre-release publicity, he never mentioned that it was based on a previously existing novel. If you didn't know otherwise, you would think that he had invented the whole story himself. Of course, this backfired on him terribly when the movie came out and flopped miserably. It opened in eight hundred theaters and the grosses were terrible, and they went down steadily and swiftly, which indicated bad word-of-mouth. So, in the sense that he wanted all the credit for it, he wound up taking all the blame. But he landed on his feet. He wound up in television producing *Miami Vice*, which got him back in the good graces of the money people.

SCHWEITZER: Has there been movie interest in any of your other works?

WILSON: Yes. *The Tomb* has been optioned twice. New World Pictures had it for a long time, but they couldn't get a good script. Then they found that somebody else had come out with another movie called *The Tomb*—it was a real dog of a movie, but they couldn't get the title then of *The Tomb*, which they wanted. So they let it drop. *The Touch* has been optioned twice, once by Stephen J. Cannell Productions for a Movie of the Week. Now, as we speak, *Sibs* has had some good reviews in *Publishers Weekly*, and there have been maybe twenty calls from production companies or studios for copies. So we'll see what happens on that. I would like to have more control next time.

SCHWEITZER: What do you find to be necessary for a successful horror story, either on film or in a book?

WILSON: Every time I try to put this into words, I read it later and say, well, no, that's wrong. It's one of those things where I know it when I see it, and I miss it when it's not there. The obvious thing to say is the human element. There has to be something to latch onto, something human to touch and to draw you along into the story. I think that without that humanity, *any* story will fail. In horror fiction, where you are stressing your characters to the extreme and you're stressing the reader as well as the characters, you need that anchor of humanity to keep the reader emotionally involved. Otherwise the gore, the violence, or whatever loses its human meaning, becomes some sort of recitation, and the reader disconnects.

Also, the thing that I demand in something that I'm reading, and also in something I'm writing, is a sense of wonder. That's usually applied to science fiction, but I think it adds an extra dimension to horror fiction, that there is something else going on, there is something wondrous out there. Even if it's horrible, it's wondrous, not mundane and tacky. That to me makes the horror more exciting, gives it a greater scope.

SCHWEITZER: You're describing something close to Lovecraft's theories of "cosmic horror." He definitely wanted a broader sense of the extra-mundane. But he didn't think that the individual characters were very important, because in the cosmic sceme of things, all individuals are dwarfed. But this seems to be the rationale for "supernatural horror," as opposed to, say, serial-killer books.

WILSON: Exactly. I think that's why Lovecraft works better in small doses than he does in large doses, because of his lack of emphasis on the human element. I find his novels tedious, but his short stories are very effective. When there is less time to develop character, you will excuse a more prefunctory or superficial job. But when you're given a lot of elbow room, the reader does expect more depth. Obviously I've been influenced by the Lovecraftian cosmic horror. I've always been impressed by the way he threw out the Judeo-Christian mythology without even saying he was throwing it out. He just dismissed it and introduced his own, which, even as a young teenager—a thirteen-year-old when I started reading him—I found very impressive. But the cosmic horror lends a definite sense of wonder that gives Lovecraft, for me, a dimension that makes him readable, even later on. I have recently gone back and reread a few of his things.

SCHWEITZER: It sounds like he was an important influence on you, but couldn't be correctly described as one of your current favorites.

WILSON: I rarely reread anybody, so the fact that I reread him at all is a testimony to his importance. I recently reread "The Thing on the Doorstep." I was doing an essay on it for a British magazine, and I really enjoyed rereading it. But I was shocked to discover that *Sibs* knocks off some of the plot elements of "The Thing on the Doorstep." I hadn't read it since 1959, but I suddenly realized that I had stolen a few things from the story. It shook me up a little because I thought I had been so wonderfully original with *Sibs*, and here I was finding out that I had already read part of it.

SCHWEITZER: We've all had that experience to some extent. The readers of *Weird Tales* know this. In issue number 296, there is a story by one Darrell Schweitzer entitled "Soft," which of course sounds remarkably like "Soft" by F. Paul Wilson, which was published a couple years earlier. And some while after this story had been published, I was looking through a copy of *Masques I*, and I thought, "Oh, shit..." Both stories have to do with people getting squishy, too, although mine achieved this in a very different manner. It had no medical realism, for instance. I couldn't very well have entitled it "Squishy." But I had read your story. I had even reviewed the book it appeared in, but I had forgotten that title, and there we were.

WILSON: There are things I have consciously swiped through the years. When I was starting out, I swiped little things from Niven and Heinlein when I was doing science fiction, concepts or little twists. Most writers start off by imitating. But you do forget, and I'm sure you file away things you like into some part of the morass in the center of your brain. Then it'll pop up in another part and you think it's all your own. But as long as it's not too blatant, I don't think anybody really minds.

SCHWEITZER: Have you always been widely read in classic horror fiction? You could then be consciously or unconsciously digging into Robert W. Chambers or Arthur Machen, or whoever. Lovecraft, for instance, had read virtually everything, and therefore was open to the influence of an enormous range of writers.

WILSON: No. I was more influenced from Lovecraft onward. That was where I did most of my reading when I could find it. In the 1950s, if you were a fan of horror fiction, it was damn hard to find anything unless you knew somebody who had old magazines. You saw a new Matheson collection now and then, the old Bradbury stuff, though he had basically stopped writing horror fiction by 1950 or so. You found a Charles Beaumont or a Dennis Wheatley, but, besides the reprint anthologies like *The Macabre Reader* or—Avon did something called *Brrrr!*—there was nothing out there. I had a big hunger for it. *Famous Monsters of Filmland* could take you just so far, and the old Gothic folks like Machen or Le Fanu didn't really cut it for me. Sure I read *Dracula* and *Frankenstein*, but the others I tried I found almost unreadable. They had no influence on me at all. I was much more influenced by the old *Weird Tales* crowd, and Matheson's *Shock* books. Some of his earlier stories just blew me away. I can still get a chill when I re-read "The Distributor." "Born of Man and Woman" still gives my heart a little tug when I reread it.

SCHWEITZER: But you didn't find all the classic, fat ghost-story anthologies like the Fraser and Wise's *Great Tales of the Supernatural* or Boris Karloff's *And the Darkness Falls*?

WILSON: I never saw them, I guess, although I did make a trip to Bermuda when I was sixteen and I came across the NOT AT NIGHT paperbacks, from Arrow, I think, with the neat, lurid covers. They were still old tales. George Fielding Eliot's "The Copper Bowl" was something that really grossed me out as a kid. Of course there were things like *The Graveyard Reader* and Basil Davenport's anthologies for Ballantine. But all of them, even *Zacherley's Midnight Snacks* and *Vulture Stew*, were from *Weird Tales* and *Unknown Worlds*. So there was nothing new happening, even in the '60s, until *Rosemary's Baby*.

SCHWEITZER: There was nothing happening in horror when you started writing? Was that what caused you to start in science fiction initially, because there wasn't a horror market?

WILSON: Yes. I read both. I read science fiction as a substitute for the horror fiction I couldn't find. I think I got into science fiction because I read the old Ray Bradbury, *The October Country*, and I liked it so much that I picked up the next Ray Bradbury book I saw and it was *The Martian Chronicles*. So I started to move into science fiction, my other love. It's always been those two genres for me. When I was seven years old, the two things I liked the most in the world were rocketships and dinosaurs. Dinosaurs represented the horror end of things, and the rocketships were science fiction. I started trying to sell my horror stories at the height of the New Wave. Where could you sell a horror story? I tried to sell them to Salmonson's *Fantasy and Terror*. I tried selling to Joseph Payne Brennan's *Macabre*. I got turned down by them.

SCHWEITZER: Did you try Robert A. W. Lowndes?

WILSON: I finally sold a semi-horror, semi-science fiction story to *Startling Mystery Stories* for the final issue. But, basically if you wanted to write something with imagination, science fiction was the only place to do it. But as soon as the horror market started opening up, I made the switch. There was no place before then that I could actually sell something like *The Keep*, which had been brewing for quite some time. It was something that I wanted to write. I had pretty much said what I had to say in science fiction. I figured I could just go on repeating myself, or I could head into new territory. So I showed a few story ideas to my agent, and he said, "Why don't we go with this castle in Romania here and see what you can do with that?" So that's how it began.

SCHWEITZER: Have you ever personally had a horrific experience which could be fodder for this sort of story?

WILSON: No. I lead a very mundane existence and I'm a hard-bound realist. I do not believe in the supernatural at all, but I do love it as a storytelling milieu, and I love to tell stories. I love to be scared. My mother sometimes told me stories that gave me a chill. She always had an aunt or someone who had seen something strange. She was rural Irish from the Berkshire area of Massachusetts, and she'd tell stories about how my aunt would see this glowing hand with a knife in it go floating down the hall past her door and continue down the hall every night. So finally she followed it to her son's room and saw it stab him in the belly. Two days later, my cousin came down with abdominal pain and went under the knife for an appendectomy. As much as those stories gave me the willies, I always used to say, "Have you got any more like that?" I've never used them, but I may use that one sometime.

SCHWEITZER: It seems that for the horror reader, the approach to this sort of material is an ambiguous mix of "If only" and "I'm glad it's not."

WILSON: Yes. In science fiction it's "If only" and "I wish it were" and definitely in horror fiction you're glad it's not. It's a safe kind of thrill in the sense that you can control it. *Any time I want, I can close this book, and I'll be okay. I won't have to see what's going on there. I can stop it.* But we don't close the book. We bought it to be scared. And after you've read the final page, you can go back to your daily existence, unscathed. Unless...unless you've been in the hands of a writer who knows his stuff, who knows how to get under the skin of the reader. A reader can always wash off the splatter, but if you've somehow been able to unsettle your reader's preconceptions, been able to worm under the skin and linger with the reader even after he or she closes the book, then I think you have done your job. You've disturbed the readers on a deeper level. You've reached them. You've made contact. I think that's what we're all trying to do.

I remember the first story I ever wrote. I only wrote half of it. I was in, I think, second grade. We had a reading circle in class and we took turns reading things. I told the teacher I had written a story myself. She was very happy and she said, "Well, do you want to read it to us?" I had only written half of it. It was a haunted house/ghost story. So I read the part I had written, and then I started ad-libbing. Within a few sentences it became obvious that I hadn't finished. The teacher was very nice, and she said, "Well Paul, when you finish it, you can come back and read the rest of it to us." I was a little embarrassed that I'd got caught, but as we were putting our chairs away from the reading circle, a couple of the kids came up to me and said, "Well what happened? What happened next?" I didn't say so in as many words, but somewhere, something inside of me came alive and said, *You've got them.* I really liked that feeling. I'd made contact. They were mine. They really wanted to know. They would have sat down right there and listened to the rest of the story. That's what we're all after. Maybe to other people it means nothing, but to me it was like a drug. I wanted to do it again and again.

SCHWEITZER: Thanks, Paul.

A SELECTED SECONDARY BIBLIOGRAPHY ON F. PAUL WILSON

Klein, J. K. "Biolog: F. Paul Wilson," in *Analog* 101 (January 5, 1981): 52.

McDonald, T. Liam. "Profiles in Terror: F. Paul Wilson," in *Cemetary Dance* 2 (Fall 1990): 14-20.]

"Prometheus Rebounds," in *Locus* 13 (December 1980/January 1981): 3.

Proulx, Kevin E. "F. Paul Wilson," in *Fear to the World: Eleven Voices in a Chorus of Horror*. Mercer Island, WA: Starmont House, 1992, p. 153-169.

Wilgus, Neal. "Interview with F. Paul Wilson," in *Science Fiction Review* 15 (August 1986): 28-30.

INDEX

ABOUT DARRELL SCHWEITZER

DARRELL SCHWEITZER is the author of two published fantasy novels: *The Shattered Goddess* (1982) and *The White Isle* (1990); with a third, *The Mask of the Sorcerer*, forthcoming. Over one hundred of his stories have appeared in many magazines and anthologies, including *Twilight Zone*, *Amazing Stories*, *Fear*, *The Year's Best Horror Stories*, *Obsessions*, *Masques IV*, *Narrow Houses*, *Scare Care*, and *Borderlands*. Some have been collected in *We Are All Legends* (1981), *Tom O'Bedlam's Night Out* (1985), and *Transients and Other Disquieting Stories* (1993).

He has written critical studies about H. P. Lovecraft and Lord Dunsany. He has edited such critical symposia as *Discovering Modern Horror Fiction I* and *II* (1985 & 1988), *Discovering H.P. Lovecraft* (1987), and *Exploring Fantasy Worlds* (1985); and, with George Scithers, the anthologies *Tales from the Spaceport Bar* and *Another Round at the Spaceport Bar*.

His reviews and columns have been a steady feature of *Aboriginal Science Fiction*, *Science Fiction Review*, *Quantum*, *The Philadelphia Inquirer*, and *The Boston Phoenix* for many years. From 1977 to 1982, he worked editorially on *Isaac Asimov's Science Fiction Magazine* (which experience provided the basis for *On Writing Science Fiction: The Editors Strike Back* with George Scithers and John M. Ford), and from 1982 to 1986, on *Amazing Stories*. As editor of *Weird Tales* he shared a World Fantasy Award with George Scithers in 1992. His novella, *To Become a Sorcerer*, was a finalist for the same award that year.

He has conducted nearly ninety author interviews, some of which have been collected in *Science Fiction Voices* (1976), *Science Fiction Voices #1* (1979), and *Science Fiction Voices #5* (1981), the latter two available from The Borgo Press. Forthcoming soon from The Borgo Press is the anthology, *Discovering Classic Fantasy*.